THE DRUIDS

THE DRUIDS

Nora K. Chadwick

New edition with foreword by
Anne Ross

CARDIFF
UNIVERSITY OF WALES PRESS
1997

First edition, 1966
Second edition, 1997. Reprinted, 2000

British Library Cataloguing in Publication Data
A catalogue record for this book is available from the British Library.

ISBN 0-7083-1435-X hardback
ISBN 0-7083-1416-3 paperback

Printed in Great Britain by Dinefwr Press, Llandybïe

To

JOCELYN M. C. TOYNBEE

in admiration of her work and
gratitude for her life-long friendship

Contents

Foreword to the Second Edition

by Anne Ross

No study of the Celts can be complete without taking into account the nature and role of the famous erudite class, the Druids, men who combined the roles of priest, philosopher, augur and teacher, the very cream of pagan Celtic society. The ancient worlds of Greece and Rome, with which they came into contact, were fascinated by them although it is not certain that they really understood their formidable powers and influence. Nevertheless, they have left us a colourful and sometimes astute record of their early reputation in the classical world. In addition to these records seen through classical eyes, there is a rich and prolific source of evidence for this learned, aristocratic class to be found buried deep in the huge corpus of vernacular literature in Irish and, to a lesser extent, in Welsh; this allows us to glimpse the Druids through Celtic eyes. Finally there is the ever-increasing weight of evidence provided by archaeology, a rapidly developing science. Devoid as it usually is of written testimony, it can, nevertheless, produce tantalizingly suggestive results from the excavations of putative temple-sites, graves and the material remains which are often recovered from such sites. Inscriptions in Greek or Gaulish or Latin are also being found by archaeological methods and these may often add testimony to what we surmise about pagan Celtic religion with which the subject of the Druids is, of course, inextricably intertwined. Votive depositions, extremely common and often lavish, can cast light on other aspects of Celtic cult practice and may, on occasion, provide evidence for the human sacrifice so graphically described by certain of the classical commentators. And, finally, as more attention is being paid to the value of folklore and surviving folk traditions, it is now possible to attempt to create a new and ever-expanding framework into which fragments of evidence may be fitted. The late John A. MacCulloch made a perceptive statement in his book *The Religion of the Ancient Celts* published in 1911. He commented: 'Druidism was not a formal system *outside* Celtic religion. It covered the whole ground of Celtic religion; in other words, it was that religion itself' (p.301). We cannot hope to have any true understanding of the Druids, Celtic religion or the nature of the Celts themselves—and their often complex and abstruse thought-processes—without appreciating this fundamental association at all periods and throughout the wider Celtic world. Religion has always been, and continues to be, of first importance to the Celtic mind, whether it be pagan or, later, Christian in belief. It is this fact that led Caesar to comment, 'the whole Gallic people is exceedingly given to religious superstition', and all the sources of evidence concur with this.

Nora Chadwick was an excellent scholar. She began her academic career by reading English, English Literature and Old English at Cambridge where she was a pupil of Hector Munro Chadwick, whom she married in 1922. It was a union that led to many fine academic achievements and ensured that Mrs Chadwick remained a scholar and prolific writer for the rest of her life. She became deeply interested in Celtic matters, learnt Old Irish and published several studies of Celtic and Welsh interest. In the latter part of her life she wrote *The Druids* which was first published in 1966, two years before the late Professor Piggott published his own elegant and erudite work on the same subject. Although the book bears an all-embracing title, it is mainly concerned with the Druids through the eyes of the classical Greek and Roman commentators. The classical sources are her prime concern and these she treats in a characteristically scholarly fashion. Professor Piggott draws attention to her perspicacity when he comments in his own *The Druids*: 'Mrs Chadwick in her recent discussion of these sources made a division of them into two groups distinguished by their chronological contents.' Of these two groups, the earlier is here called the 'Posidonian' tradition, written in the first century BC, which is often critical of the Celts. The second group is labelled the 'Alexandrian' tradition, dating mainly from the first century AD onwards but containing earlier material as well. This group takes a more idealistic view of the Druids and their background, an approach known as 'soft primitivism' to historians of ideas. Mrs Chadwick has written a most useful and scholarly book, which is a valuable guide to the classical attitudes to the Druids.

It is nevertheless very much a product of its time, and it is not now possible to agree with all her conclusions. Of these, two must be mentioned here. The first is, as Professor Kenneth Jackson puts it in his obituary notice for Nora Chadwick, which was published in the year of her death (*Proceedings of the British Academy*, LVIII, 1972): '*The Druids* is . . . partly a collection of the facts and partly speculations about them; notably a theory, to which she obstinately clung, that the Druids were not priests.' And Piggott comments in his own *The Druids* (p. 108):

> In view of a recently-expressed opinion that the Druids should not rightly be called priests . . . despite Mrs Chadwick's pleading, it seems impossible to use these terms (priest, priesthood) without including Druids with the other named functionaries . . . and the doubtless numerous grades whose names have not been preserved, within a Celtic priesthood. A class of learned men, repositories of the traditional wisdom of the tribe whether it concerned the gods or men; the way to write a poem or construct a calendar; the due rite of sacrifice and the correct interpretations of omens—this is a priesthood, and the Druids are an integral part of it, both in the classical and the vernacular sources.

The second point, which must be particularly frustrating to Celtic scholars, is Mrs Chadwick's denial of druidic ideas and concepts as having any great value in their own right, being merely 'the outer ripple on the circumference from the great centres of thought elsewhere' (p. 57). This attitude has been noted by other scholars including Professor D. Ellis Evans in his long and masterly review of the book (*Llên Cymru*, 9, 1966, 119–23).

Nevertheless, Mrs Chadwick's scholarly and critical study will take its place beside other classics such as Sir Thomas Kendrick's great work, *The Druids*, published in 1927, and Professor Piggott's learned and elegant study, *The Druids*, published in 1968.

Finally, Mrs Chadwick is to be praised for the very useful and comprehensive *Alphabetical List of the Principal Classical References* with which the book begins and which is an invaluable help to the reader.

Further Reading

Since the publication of Nora Chadwick's *The Druids* in 1966 there have been only two major studies of the Druids, Stuart Piggott's *The Druids* (Thames and Hudson, 1968), which I have already mentioned, and *Les Druides* by F. Le Roux and Guyonvarc'h (Editions Ouest-France, Rennes, 1986).

Developments in the last three decades in the science of archaeology have led to new speculations about the nature of Celtic society and religion. For Ireland it is of value to study Barry Raftery's *Pagan Celtic Ireland* (Thames and Hudson, 1994), and his comments add a new dimension to the sites we have included on the map. I must also mention Jean Louis Brunaux's important study, *The Celtic Gauls* (1987; English translation, B. A. Seaby, 1988) for its discussion of recently discovered sanctuary sites and their excavations, and his more general discussion of Celtic religion and society. Likewise David Rankin's important study, *Celts and the Classical World* (Croom Helm, 1987), a classicist's view of the wider Celtic world, which includes a chapter on 'Religion and the Druids'. For sacrificial offerings, including human sacrifices, votive hoards and ritual deposits, it is useful to consult an excellent study by Richard Bradley, *The Passage of Arms* (Cambridge University Press, 1990). Coming to a wider discussion of some Irish literary material in which there are several references to 'druidry', Kim McCone's *Pagan Past and Christian Present in Early Irish Literature* (An Sagart, Maynooth Monographs, 1991) is stimulating and at times controversial. For druidic ritual, see Anne Ross, 'Ritual and the Druids', in Miranda Green (ed.), *The Celtic World* (Routledge, 1995).

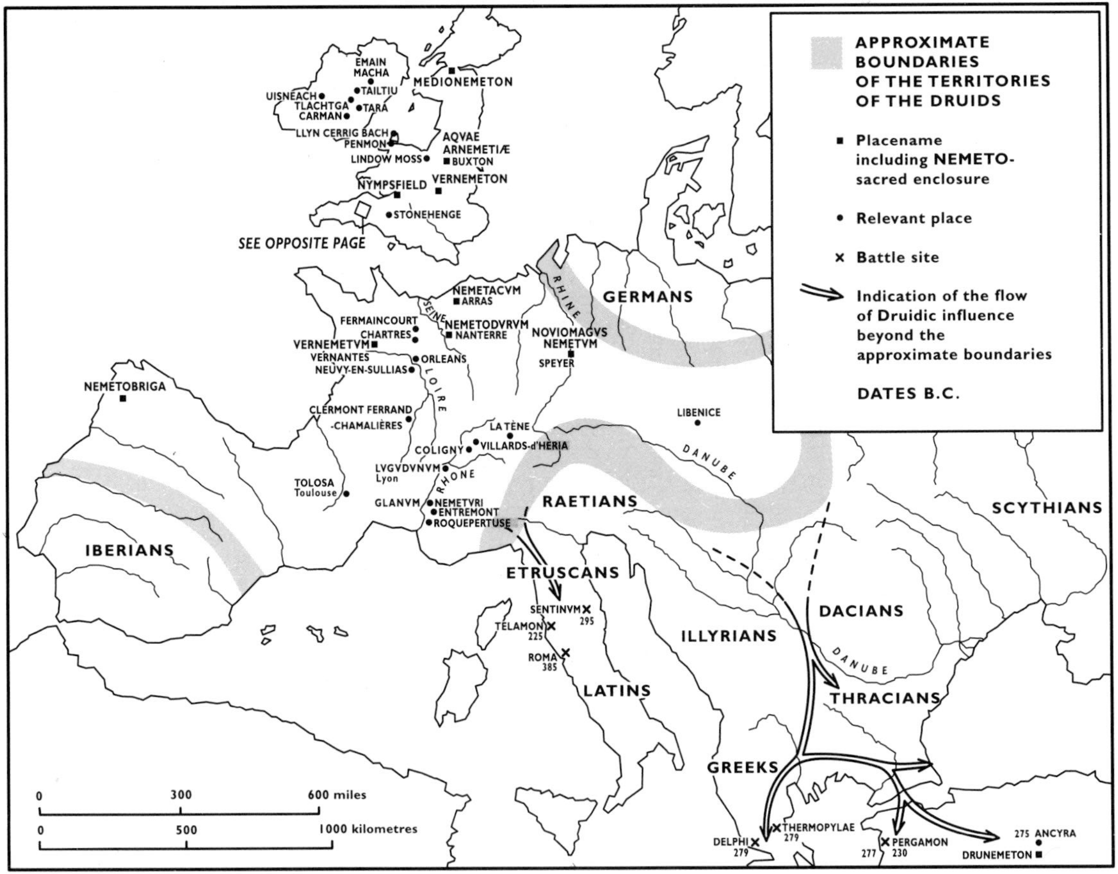
APPROXIMATE BOUNDARIES OF THE TERRITORIES OF THE DRUIDS
Placename including NEMETO- sacred enclosure
Relevant place
Battle site
Indication of the flow of Druidic influence beyond the approximate boundaries
DATES B.C.
EMAIN MACHA
MEDIONEMETON
UISNEACH
TAILTIU
TLACHTGA
TARA
CARMAN
LLYN CERRIG BACH
PENMON
AQVAE ARNEMETIÆ
BUXTON
LINDOW MOSS
NYMPSFIELD
VERNEMETON
STONEHENGE
SEE OPPOSITE PAGE
NEMETACVM
ARRAS
SEINE
NEMETODVRVM
NANTERRE
FERMAINCOURT
CHARTRES
VERNEMETVM
VERNANTES
ORLEANS
NEUVY-EN-SULLIAS
LOIRE
NOVIOMAGVS NEMETVM
SPEYER
RHINE
GERMANS
NEMETOBRIGA
CLERMONT FERRAND -CHAMALIÈRES
LA TÈNE
COLIGNY
VILLARDS-d'HERIA
LIBENICE
DANUBE
LVGVDVNVM Lyon
RHONE
TOLOSA Toulouse
GLANVM
NEMETVRI
ENTREMONT
ROQUEPERTUSE
RAETIANS
SCYTHIANS
IBERIANS
ETRUSCANS
SENTINVM 295
TELAMON 225
ROMA 385
DACIANS
ILLYRIANS
DANUBE
LATINS
THRACIANS
GREEKS
DELPHI 279
THERMOPYLAE 279
277 PERGAMON 230
275 ANCYRA
DRUNEMETON
0 300 600 miles
0 500 1000 kilometres

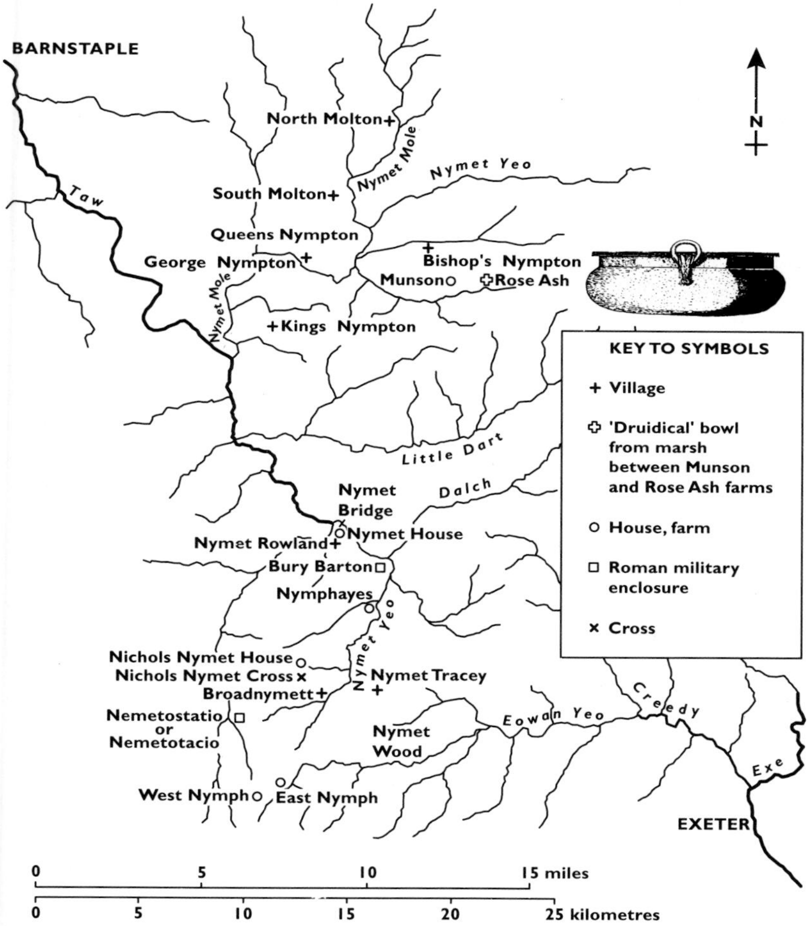
BARNSTAPLE
Taw
North Molton
Nymet Mole
Nymet Yeo
South Molton
Queens Nympton
George Nympton
Bishop's Nympton
Munson
Rose Ash
Nymet Mole
Kings Nympton
KEY TO SYMBOLS
+ Village
'Druidical' bowl from marsh between Munson and Rose Ash farms
○ House, farm
□ Roman military enclosure
× Cross
N
Little Dart
Nymet Bridge
Dalch
Nymet House
Nymet Rowland
Bury Barton
Nymphayes
Nymet Yeo
Nichols Nymet House
Nichols Nymet Cross
Nymet Tracey
Broadnymett
Creedy
Nemetostatio or Nemetotacio
Eowan Yeo
Nymet Wood
Exe
West Nymph
East Nymph
EXETER
0 5 10 15 miles
0 5 10 15 20 25 kilometres

NEMETO-, NYMET, NYMP- names in the TAW valley, Devonshire, England

Note on Maps

Map 1

This map indicates a selection of sites and centres in Ireland, Britain, continental Europe and Turkey which are associated with the Druids.

In Ireland, the main sites were the druidical centre, Uisneach, the ceremonial centre, Emain Macha, the royal centre Tara and the *oenaich*, assembly sites. In Britain, the most significant were the putative druidical centre, Penmon, and the offering site Llyn-cerrig-bach, both in Môn (Anglesey); Lindow Moss; Stonehenge; and the Nemeton sites. In Gaul, the marked sites are the Nemeton sites; the druidical centre, Fermaincourt; the calendar sites, Coligny and Villard-d'Heria; the sanctuary sites in the lower Rhône region; Chamalières; Toulouse—Aurum Tolosarum. In Hungary, the sacred enclosure, Libenice, should be noted; in Turkey, Drunemeton in Galatia. The expansion of the Celts through the Balkans to Turkey and into the Italian peninsula is indicated by arrows.

Map 2

This map indicates the Nemeton sites in the Taw valley, Devonshire.

Preface

THE druids are the most advanced of all intellectual classes among the peoples of ancient Europe beyond the Greek and Roman world. They are the most distinguished members of the Celtic communities of Gaul. The institution of druidism, referred to by Caesar as their *disciplina*, never failed to capture the imagination of the ancient world. Its impact on the modern world is hardly less impressive, as can be deduced from the steady flow of studies devoted to the druids published in all the principal countries. The fascination of the subject is everlasting.

Two reasons may be suggested for this perennial appeal. The first is the attraction of the unknown. Despite the fact that for close on a thousand years ancient Greek and Roman writers interested themselves in inquiring into, and reporting upon the druids, we are still very much in the dark. Almost all that has come down to us has been information received at second or third hand, apparently from a period when the druids had long been in their decline, and their *disciplina* had entered upon a period of disintegration, and when their subversive political influence, however limited in effect, had coloured the Roman reports which have survived.

But the chief reason for the perennial attraction of the druids is inherent in the subject itself. This is the paramount interest which must always attach itself to a class of people who have cultivated and transmitted a 'system' of thought without the aid of writing. Without claiming for the druids any coherent philosophical system and without denying that in some of their practical responsibilities they were implicated in those institutions of the Gauls among whom they lived and functioned which were relics of primitive barbarity, we cannot fail to be impressed by their preoccupation with spiritual and intellectual matters.

It is, in fact, this deep concern with spiritual and intellectual matters which constitutes the chief lasting claim of the druids on our attention. Education was in their hands, and rarely has it been carried on with more sustained and prolonged assiduity. Rarely has it been devoted to matters less utilitarian or more majestic. Their central subjects were nature and the Universe; their leading doctrine, the immortality of the soul.

That they were philosophers rather than priests there can, in my mind, be no doubt. Nothing in our accounts suggests a priesthood. The word 'priest' is never applied to them. There is no central organization such as one associates with a sacerdotal body. No clear evidence points to their connexion with either temples or formal, established sanctuaries, or to liturgy or prayers conducted by them. Negative evidence indeed implies that routine sacerdotal functions were outside their sphere of activities.

In our past efforts to understand the nature, the functions, and the history of the druids we have over-simplified the subject, treating their range and period as if both were static, viewing them in two dimensions, omitting the relative chronology and the stemmata of our sources of information. This omission of the third dimension has seriously distorted the picture. In the following brief study I have attempted to unpick the evidence as this had been handed down to us from the ancient world, and I have sought to trace the evidence from the earliest times in Gaul, where druids were first known, and where they chiefly flourished, from the height of their power till their decline.

The decline of the druids! This has been a battle-ground among all scholars who have seriously studied the druids and their place in antiquity. Why did the Romans 'repress', 'persecute', 'abolish' the druids? Pliny was the first to raise the question, and he answered it with assurance to his own satisfaction. Nevertheless the question has been re-opened and re-studied ever since. This has been, in fact, the burning question in our own day for students of the Roman Empire and the Celtic West alike. It is the question which first prompted me to attempt the present study.

My conclusion is that the 'repression' and 'persecution' of the druids by the Romans is to a very considerable extent a creation of later scholarship, seeking a rational basis for the disappearance of this ancient and important Gaulish institution. This widespread belief in the 'abolishment' is not wholly without warrant, as I have shown below. On the whole, however, the evidence for suppression is not very impressive. No Roman legislation against the druids has come down to us, and no first-class contemporary evidence testifies to repressive measures. The broad answer would seem to be that the *disciplina* of the druids perished by slow strangulation, the inevitable result of the superimposition of a higher culture on a lower. The effective implementation of the Roman administrative system inevitably stifled the old-world traditional culture of Celtic Gaul. The bell which announced the opening of the first session of the Roman university of Augustodunum sounded the death-knell of the oral druidical schools of Bibracte, and drove their teachers to the backwoods.

I suppose that no one has ever come to the end of his book without a remorseful feeling that if he were to begin again he would write it quite differently. This is the measure of his own profit from the task which he has completed, however deficient its value may prove to be to his readers. This must be my apologia for the errors and inadequacy of the present work, despite the generous help which I have received from my brilliant friends. In particular I am grateful to F. H. Sandbach of Trinity College, Cambridge; to Professor J. E. Caerwyn Williams of Bangor, North Wales, and to Professor Idris Ll. Foster of Oxford, all of whom read my book in manuscript; to Professor J. M. C. Toynbee, to Joyce M. Reynolds of Newnham College, Cambridge, and to Joan E. A. Liversidge of Cambridge, who have read the proofs and made many helpful comments; and to Mr. R. E. Thompson for preparing the Index. I need hardly add that I alone am responsible for such errors as may remain.

Finally I would add my gratitude to the University of Wales for undertaking the publication of my book, and to their staff and to the staff of the University Press, Oxford, who have printed it on their behalf, for the care which they have bestowed on its production. In particular I would wish to add my special thanks to the proof-reader whose expert and meticulous care has saved me from many errors.

Cambridge, 1965 — Nora K. Chadwick

Alphabetical List of the Principal Classical References

EXTRACTS from Classical authors relating to Gaul will be found in the following works:

M. Bouquet, *Rerum Gallicarum et Francicarum Scriptores: Recueil des historiens des Gaules et de la France.* Tome I (Paris, 1738). New ed., published under the direction of M. Léopold Delisle, Paris, 1869.

E. Cougny, *Γαλλικῶν Συγγραφεῖς Ἑλληνικοί: Extraits des auteurs grecs concernant la géographie et l'histoire des Gaules* (Texte et traduction nouvelle), Tome I (Paris, 1878). For important comments on Cougny's unsatisfactory chronological arrangement, see the work by H. d'Arbois de Jubainville cited below, pp. x–xiii.

H. d'Arbois de Jubainville, *Principaux auteurs de l'antiquité à consulter sur l'histoire des Celtes depuis les temps les plus anciens jusqu'au règne de Théodose 1er* (Paris, 1902).

W. Dinan, *Monumenta Historica Celtica*: Notices of the Celts in the Writings of Greek and Latin Authors from the Tenth Century B.C. to the Fifth Century A.D., arranged chronologically, with English translations, Vol. I (London, 1911).

J. Zwicker, *Fontes Historiae Religionis Celticae*, Pars I (Berlin, 1934); Pars II (1935); Pars III with Index (1936).

The editions which I have chiefly used are the *Bibliotheca Scriptorum Graecorum et Romanorum* in the series published by B. G. Teubner of Leipzig, diplomatic edition; the *Collection des Universités de France* publiée sous le patronage de l'Association Guillaume Budé, text, with introduction, commentary, and French translation; and the *Loeb Classical Library*, published at London by W. Heinemann; at New York by G. P. Putnam's Sons; and at Cambridge, Massachusetts by the

Harvard University Press, with Introduction, commentary, and English translation.

It is hoped that the following list of classical authors referred to in the succeeding chapters may be of convenience to readers, and will reduce the necessity of chronological discussions in the text.

Those authors whose works are written in Greek are indicated by an asterisk *, those in Latin thus, †.

These notes are based on entries in classical dictionaries, chiefly the *Oxford Classical Dictionary* (Oxford, 1950, reprint), and Smith's *Classical Dictionary* (London, 1894), and in Pauly–Wissowa, *Real-Encyclopädie der klassischen Altertumswissenschaft* (Stuttgart, 1894–), cited below as Pauly–Wissowa, *R.-E.* To all of these I offer grateful acknowledgement.

AGATHARCHIDES* (*fl.* in second half of c. II B.C.), a Greek scholar and Peripatetic philosopher, born at Cnidos, lived in Alexandria. Wrote a number of historical and geographical works of which only fragments and an epitome of a work on the Erythraean Sea remain, containing an account of the Red Sea coasts (*c.* 110 B.C.), partly reproduced by Diodorus Siculus (q.v.), &c.

AMMIANUS MARCELLINUS† (*c.* A.D. 330–91 or later), considered to be the last of the great Roman historians. He wrote of the period A.D. 96–378. He appears to have been in Gaul with Ursicinus with whom he had served in the East. He is an important authority on the druids, having obtained his material from much earlier sources, among whom he cites Timagenes (q.v.) with deep respect.

ANACHARSIS* (*c.* 600 B.C.), a hellenized Scythian widely travelled in Asia Minor and Greece, and renowned for his wisdom. Traditionally regarded, from the fourth century B.C., as one of the 'Seven Sages'.

APOLLODORUS* (*fl. c.* 140 B.C.), first of Alexandria and later of Athens, a 'grammarian' and Stoic of wide interests, and author of many books now lost, including one on mythology and heroic legend, which survives only in a much later summary; a metrical *Chronica* narrating world history from the fall of Troy; the *Περὶ θεῶν*, an account of Greek religion; the important commentary on the Homeric Catalogue of Ships based on earlier works, and used later by Strabo.

ATHENAEUS* (*fl. c.* A.D. 200), a scholar of Naucratis in Egypt, who lived later at Alexandria and Athens. The *Δειπνοσοφισταί* ('The Learned at Dinner'), probably completed after A.D. 192, is his only extant work, of which fifteen books out of a probable thirty survive. The framework is that of a Symposium at which the guests are 'learned doctors' who discourse on a wide variety of subjects at a banquet extending over several days.

CELSUS* wrote (*c.* A.D. 178–80) 'The True Discourse' (*Ἀληθὴς λόγος*) the earliest literary attack on Christianity, largely quoted in the famous reply by Origen (q.v.), *Contra Celsum*. Celsus wrote from the point of view of a Greek Platonist, but incorporated and apparently accepted certain arguments against Christianity which he attributes to the Jews in Egypt. The work is of great importance as illustrating the Greek attitude of the day to Christianity, and for its knowledge of certain sects, notably the Gnostics.

CICERO† (106–43 B.C.), orator, author, letter-writer, and the greatest Latin prose stylist. His chief residences were first in Rome and later in his villa at Tusculum, but he studied in Rhodes where he had known Posidonius (q.v.).

CLEMENT OF ALEXANDRIA* (*c.* A.D. 150–between 211 and 216), a Greek Christian theologian with a wide knowledge of Greek literature and Stoic philosophy, who was converted to Christianity and who taught in Alexandria. Among his surviving works is the *Stromateis* (commonly referred to by modern writers as *Stromata*), 'Miscellanies', of which eight books survive. Among his sources was Apollodorus (q.v.), and he also cites Timaeus (q.v.) and Alexander Cornelius

Polyhistor (q.v.). He tells us in *Stromateis* i. 11 that among his teachers one had been an Ionian, others were from southern Italy, Coele-Syria, Egypt, and the East. Of the latter one had been an Assyrian, one a Hebrew of Palestine. St. Jerome declared that he was the most learned of all the Fathers (*Epist.* lxx. 4).

CYRIL OF ALEXANDRIA* (Archbishop in A.D. 412–44). In *Contra Julianum* iv (ed. Migne, *P.G.* ix, col. 705) he cites Alexander Cornelius Polyhistor's work *De Symbolis Pythagoricis* as his justification for accepting certain philosophers known to barbarian peoples, among them the druids of Gaul.

DIO CHRYSOSTOM* (*c.* A.D. 40–after 112), an eminent Greek sophist and rhetorician under the Roman Empire, grandfather of the historian Dio Cassius. He was born near Mount Olympus, and came to Rome under Vespasian. He was banished from Italy under Domitian and wandered in Thrace and Scythia and the land of the Getae, but was reinstated in favour later under Nerva and Trajan. Eighty of his orations or essays on politics and philosophy have survived. He became a convert to Stoicism in later life. Among his lost works were attacks on philosophers and also on the Emperor Domitian.

DIODORUS SICULUS* (*fl.* under both Julius Caesar and Augustus, and lived till at least 21 B.C.). He wrote a World History (*Βιβλιοθήκη*) in forty books in which, among a host of other writers, he cites Timaeus (q.v.) and Posidonius (q.v.).

DIOGENES LAERTIUS* (*fl. c.* the second quarter of c. III A.D.). He was the author of a compendium of biographical material in ten books, still extant, generally known as the *Lives of the Philosophers*. Despite careless and uncritical elements the work is of priceless value because most of the ancient sources used by him have now been entirely lost. His information is given for the most part at second or third hand, but very often with the names of the original authorities cited. He almost certainly made use of Apollodorus (q.v.) and from time to time borrowed material from Polyhistor (q.v.). He cites both Sotion of Alexandria (q.v.) and also the *Magicus* of the Pseudo-Aristotle on the druids.

HIPPOLYTUS* (*c.* A.D. 170–*c.* 236), an important Christian writer of the second half of the second and the beginning of the third century, probably resident in Rome though his writings are in Greek. Of his work only fragments remain, the most important being the *Philosophumena*, the 'Refutation of all Heresies' in ten books, of which the second and third are lost. He is regarded as one of the most important of the theologians of the third century in the West, but although he took an active part in the controversies of the time little is known of his life.

JULIUS CAESAR† (102–44 B.C.), our fullest source for the druids. See especially *De Bello Gallico* ('The War against Gaul'), Book vi. 13, 14, 16, 18, 21.

LACTANTIUS PLACIDUS† (a grammarian of the fifth or sixth century A.D.). The glossary which survives under his name consists in reality of two separate works, one based on marginal notes in copies of early poets of the Roman Republic.

LAMPRIDIUS and VOPISCUS,† two authors whose work is included in the document known as the *Historia Augusta*, a compilation believed to be substantially of third-century date, but containing some older material, perhaps with further additions in the fourth century (cf. p. 81 below).

LIVY† (59 B.C.–A.D. 17). One of the greatest Roman historians; born at Padua, where he died; but he spent much of his time in Rome in the highest literary circles. He wrote a history of Rome in 142 books, of which 35 only are extant, and some fragments and brief epitomes of certain further sections.

LUCAN† (*c.* A.D. 39–65). A Roman poet of Spanish origin, and nephew of Lucius Annaeus Seneca. He was educated in

Rome and was appointed quaestor under Nero and a member of the college of augurs, and became a voluminous poet and writer, and a highly distinguished rhetor, with some training in Stoic philosophy. His only surviving poem (incomplete) is commonly known as the *Pharsalia*, an epic poem in ten books narrating the contest between Caesar and the Senate, and bearing in the manuscripts the title *De Bello Civili*. Convicted of conspiracy against Nero he was forced to die, and the *Pharsalia* was never finished. His chief source was Livy, but he was probably also indebted to Caesar or one of his sources.

MARTIAL† (*c.* A.D. 40–*c.* 104), an epigrammatic poet, born at Bilbilis in Spain, went to Rome in 64, and secured the patronage of Titus and Domitian. He mixed freely in high social and in literary circles. His epigrams are distinguished not only by their wit and grace, but still more by their wide humanity, and keen observation of men and manners.

MAXIMUS TYRIUS* (*c.* A.D. 125–85), a Greek sophist and lecturer in Athens and Rome and author of forty-one extant *Διαλέξεις* ('lectures'). He was without philosophical originality, but was well read in Greek literature, quoting largely from Plato and Homer.

ORIGEN* (*c.* A.D. 186–255). His life is known to us chiefly from Eusebius. He was probably born in Alexandria, of pagan parents. Here he succeeded Clement (q.v.) at the age of eighteen as a teacher of Christian philosophy when Clement fled from Alexandria on the persecution of Severus (202–3). Origen himself was forced to leave Alexandria and after much travelling settled in Caesarea *c.* 231 or soon after, where he established another school. From 231 onwards he wrote many works, including *Contra Celsum*, written *c.* 249, in eight books, which preserves about nine-tenths of the 'True Discourse' by Celsus himself (q.v.).

PLINY THE ELDER† (A.D. 23 or 24–79). He held the procuratorship in Gallia Narbonensis and Gallia Belgica. His chief and only surviving work is his *Naturalis Historia*. It consists of prefatory matter and thirty-six books, containing compendia of various geographical, ethnological, medical, and scientific subjects, gathered from a wide variety of written sources, chiefly Roman and Greek. Among these are references to Varro and Alexander Cornelius Polyhistor (q.v.), the latter of whom he cites on historical geography (iii. 16; vii. 67) and as an authority on oak-trees, mistletoe (xiii. 22), and acorns (xvi. 6). Pliny's work includes important notices on the druids.

POLYHISTOR (ALEXANDER CORNELIUS)* (born *c.* 105 B.C.), a voluminous Greek writer, and industrious collector of facts. Among his many other works he wrote a compendium, or 'history' of the philosophical schools (*Φιλοσόφων διαδοχαί*) from which Diogenes Laertius (q.v.) borrowed from time to time. He is also cited by Pliny (q.v.), by Stephanus of Byzantium (q.v.), &c. He also wrote an interpretation of Pythagorean symbols (*Περὶ Πυθαγορικῶν συμβόλων*), in which he claims to be citing from 'Pythagorean note-books' handed down from the last generation of the Pythagorean society which came to an end in the fourth century. The date of these is a subject of controversy. For some details and recent references see W. K. C. Guthrie, *A History of Greek Philosophy* (Cambridge, 1962), p. 201, n. 3. For a fuller note on Polyhistor see Pauly–Wissowa, *R.-E.*, vol. i, col. 449, s.v. *Alexandros*, no. 88. For the extant texts of Polyhistor see F. Jacoby, *Die Fragmente der Griechischen Historiker* (*F. Gr. Hist.*) (Leiden, 1940), part IIIA, no. 273. See especially Fragment 94 (138), p. 118. The chief ancient authority on Polyhistor is Diogenes Laertius (q.v.) viii. 24 ff.

POMPONIUS MELA† (*fl. c.* A.D. 43), wrote *De Chorographia*, a brief geographical survey of the world in three books, the third of which includes the outer coasts of Gaul and Brittany. The text was published by C. Frick (Leipzig, 1880).

POSIDONIUS* (*c.* 135–*c.* 50 B.C.), perhaps the most important Stoic philosopher and ethnographer of his time. He was born on the Orontes, studied philosophy at Athens, and became a teacher at Rhodes, where he was known to Cicero. He travelled widely and made scientific investigations in many of the coasts of the Western Mediterranean countries, including Gaul. His written *Histories* have perished, but much of their content has been reflected in the work of his successors.

SOPATER OF PAPHOS,* a Greek parodist and writer of farcical burlesques, who flourished in Alexandria. His dates are uncertain but he is stated to have been born in the time of Alexander the Great and he lived to mention Ptolemy II.

SOTION OF ALEXANDRIA* (*fl.* 200–170 B.C.), a Peripatetic philosopher, who wrote an account of the philosophers in the different schools (*Διαδοχὴ τῶν φιλοσόφων*) in thirteen or twenty-three books which was one main source of Diogenes Laertius (q.v.) for his *Lives of the Philosophers* (perhaps not direct however), and also, incidentally, for his knowledge of the druids.

STATIUS† (*c.* A.D. 45–96), a famous poet, born at Naples, lived in Rome where he frequented the court of Domitian. He wrote a number of poems which have survived. The best known are the *Silvae* in five books, consisting of a collection of thirty-two occasional poems addressed to his friends; and the *Thebais*, an epic in twelve books, composed on the story of the 'Seven against Thebes'.

STEPHANUS OF BYZANTIUM* (*fl.* ? early C. VII), a teacher in the court schools of Byzantium. He was author of a valuable geographical dictionary entitled *'Εθνικά* (*Ethnica*), based on and citing works of ancient authors; but only a small fragment remains. One of his favourite sources was Strabo (q.v.). He also cites Polyhistor (q.v.) frequently, but through intermediaries (cf., e.g., Orosius, *Ethnica*, ed. A. Westermann, Leipzig, 1839, p. 49). See further Pauly–Wissowa, *R.-E.*, 2nd series, vol. iii. 2, col. 2384.

STRABO* (probably *c.* 63 B.C.–after A.D. 21), a Greek geographer, historian, and an adherent of the Stoics. He had known Posidonius (q.v.). He was in Rome 44–35, *c.* 31, and 7 B.C. and had a great admiration for the Roman Empire. He may have written under the patronage of politicians or officials. His historical books are lost, but his important *Geographia* in seventeen books has survived.

SUETONIUS† (lived in the first half of the second century A.D.), a Roman historian, contemporary with Tacitus. His chief work is the *Lives of the Twelve Caesars* (including Julius).

TACITUS† (*c.* A.D. 55–120), a distinguished Roman historian, married the daughter of Agricola in 77. His *Dialogus* was probably composed after A.D. 96, his treatise *De Origine et Situ Germanorum* (commonly referred to as *Germania*) in 98. His bias is strongly in favour of the barbarian nations. His historical works consist of the so-called *Histories* (beginning with the year 64), and the *Annals*, both fragmentary.

TIMAEUS* (*c.* 356–*c.* 260 B.C.), a Greek historian and ethnographer, who compiled a voluminous work in at least 33 books chiefly on Sicilian history down to 320 B.C., preserved only in fragments. He was used extensively as an authority by subsequent historians, especially Diodorus Siculus (q.v.), Diogenes Laertius (q.v.), and Clement of Alexandria (q.v.), and his history was recognized as an authoritative storehouse by Alexandrian scholars and poets, and his collection of ethnographical facts and local legends is of unique value.

TIMAGENES*, an Alexandrian captured and brought to Rome in 55 B.C., where he was freed and became a successful teacher of rhetoric, and also an historian under Augustus. The result was a 'History of the Kings', *Βασιλεῖς*; but having fallen into disfavour with Augustus he burnt his historical books and left Rome, first for Tusculum, and later for Mesopotamia, where he died. He had collected many traditions relating to the Gauls, and is cited as an authority on the druids by Diodorus Siculus (q.v.) and Ammianus Marcellinus (q.v.). For a discussion of the extent of his later influence see R. Laqueur, in Pauly–Wissowa, *R.-E.*, 2nd series (Stuttgart, 1936), vol. vi, cols. 1063 ff.

VALERIUS FLACCUS† (died *c.* A.D. 92 or 93), author of an epic poem, the *Argonautica*, probably begun in A.D. 80. The poem (incomplete) relates the voyage of the Argonauts to Colchis.

VALERIUS MAXIMUS† (*fl.* in the first century A.D.), a Roman historian who wrote a handbook for rhetoricians, *Factorum ac Dictorum Memorabilium Libri IX*, consisting of a collection of illustrative historical anecdotes. The book is dedicated to Tiberius and is strongly nationalistic in tone, emphasizing the superiority of the Romans to all other peoples of the world. He made use of Livy (q.v.) and Cicero (q.v.) among other sources, but is uncritical in the use of his material.

VOPISCUS, see LAMPRIDIUS.

I

The Problem · Some recent studies

THE interest attaching to the druids has never failed to attract the attention of students of Celtic civilization. From at least as early as the second century B.C., and indeed much earlier, they have been the subject of comment by Classical writers, sometimes hostile, sometimes favourable. The interest of the subject has never flagged and the enthusiasm was particularly lively among the Greeks of Alexandria who in the Christian era were deeply interested in the Barbarians and their native 'wisdom'. In the words of the French historian, Camille Jullian, commenting on this perennial interest in the druids: 'Il dure toujours.'[1]

Early Classical opinion as represented by Posidonius and later writers believed to be indebted to him—Diodorus Siculus, Strabo, Caesar, Pomponius Mela, Lucan—is more reserved than the Alexandrian. On the other hand, the exaltation of the druids appears already in Alexander Cornelius Polyhistor, who was probably already flourishing as a younger contemporary of Posidonius, and to whom Diogenes Laertius was possibly, and Clement and Cyril of Alexandria were certainly, indebted. This exaltation of the druids was perhaps shared by Timagenes in a younger generation than Polyhistor. It has indeed been suggested that perhaps Polyhistor and Timagenes are the true authors of the 'legend' of the wisdom and greatness of the druids,[2] traces of which survived in the Middle Ages and reappear in popular opinion from the beginning of the Renaissance.[3]

[1] *Histoire de la Gaule* (Paris, 1908), ii. 85 f. [2] Jullian, loc. cit. 86, n. 1.

[3] Cf. e.g. A. L. Owen, *The Famous Druids* (Oxford, 1962), *passim*. On this book see the review by Professor Stewart Piggott, *Antiquity*, no. 144 (1962), p. 311.

In 1908 Camille Jullian devoted a chapter to the druids in his history of Gaul,[1] and his comprehensive list of references, especially to the Classical authorities, given in this scholarly work serves as a valuable starting-point for serious modern investigations of the druids in relation to the history of Gaul. During the half century which has passed since Jullian wrote, our knowledge of the actual number of sources for the study of the druids has not greatly increased, but considerable progress has been made in the study of the literary nature of such sources as we possess and the relative value of their authority. In addition we have learnt a larger measure of humility in their interpretation. Some modern scholars hesitate to accept Jullian's uncritical definition of the druids as 'priests',[2] as we understand the term today. In fact the term *sacerdos* does not seem to have been used of the druids by any ancient writer. The modern scholar also hesitates to accept some of Jullian's conclusions, which at times appear subjective. Much of the latter part of his study consists, in fact, of conjecture and deduction which today we would regard as arbitrary. Nevertheless his work is a sane and essentially a solid contribution to the subject.

In 1927 a book devoted to the druids was published by T. D. Kendrick.[3] This book was the first general survey of the subject which had appeared in English in modern times, and all students readily acknowledge our debt to its meticulous presentation of the chief Classical sources. The book is especially useful to English students in that a valuable Appendix brings together the texts of the chief passages from Classical authors relating to the druids, and English translations of these passages are given by Kendrick himself in chapter iii of the book.

Works on the druids are now continuing to appear in rapid

[1] *Histoire de la Gaule*, vol. ii, chap. iv, pp. 85 ff.

[2] On this term contrast E. MacNeill, *Early Irish Laws and Institutions* (Dublin, 1935), pp. 67 f. Cf. also pp. 5 ff., 97, n. 2 below.

[3] *The Druids, A Study in Keltic Prehistory* (London, 1927).

succession.[1] Among recent scholarly studies is a careful series of articles by Emile Bachelier who gives a brief up-to-date survey of the subject from the extant Classical sources.[2] The work has the signal merit of treating the history of the druids, in addition to the chronology of the sources, as an organic sequence, distinguishing sharply the evidence for druids before the Conquest of Gaul from that after the Conquest, and finally from the extant evidence for druids in the fourth century A.D.

A brief scholarly study of certain aspects of druidism was published in 1960 by Jan de Vries.[3] He assumes throughout that the druids were priests and he discusses their educational activities and teaching, their organization, and their origin. His conclusion is that they were directly derived from the priesthood of early Indo-European times, analogous to the Brahmins of India, and that their organization must have had great influence on religion and mythology from generation to generation.

Among the most considerable recent works on the druids are two brief studies by Françoise Le Roux. The first is an article 'Contribution à une définition des Druides',[4] which is of value for its survey of recent works on the subject, and for the balanced and judicial discussion of their contents, thus serving as a firm starting-point for further research. The second work by the same author is a small but careful book[5] which attempts a fresh survey of the evidence for druidism, in close association not only with early Classical references to the druids, but also with a selection of the most important passages in early Irish literary sources relating to the druids of ancient Ireland. The presentation is well in advance of most modern studies of the subject, and though the

1 Among others reference may be made to J. L. T. C. Spence, *The History and Origins of Druidism* (London, 1929).

2 *Ogam*, xi (1959), pp. 46 ff., 173 ff., 295 ff.; xii (1960), pp. 91 ff. A brief general summary of the subject was published by E. MacNeill, op. cit., chap. iii. See especially pp. 66 ff.

3 'Die Druiden', *Kairos*, ii. 67 ff.

4 *Ogam*, xii (1960), pp. 475 ff.

5 *Les Druides* (Paris, 1961).

critical treatment leaves something to be desired, the student will profit by a careful reading of the rich store of material here offered for comparative purposes. A fresh beginning has here been made in the use of the Celtic literary evidence for druids as they appear in the earliest literature of ancient Ireland.

Some scholarly studies have appeared in recent years on special aspects of the druids and the problems to which they give rise. An important recent inquiry into the reason for the suppression of the druids by the Romans was introduced in a lecture delivered by the late Professor Hugh Last of Oxford during the Congress of Classical Societies held at Oxford in 1948, and subsequently published in 1949 in vol. xxxix of the *Journal of Roman Studies* under the title of 'Rome and the Druids: A Note'. Professor Last's study is written frankly as a contribution to a controversy which has continued over a long period of years among scholars and historians as to the Roman policy in regard to the conquered barbarian countries within the Empire. Last refers to the views of modern scholars as to whether the object of the Romans in suppressing druidism was political or cultural, and he reopens the debate: 'Was the consideration which brought Rome into conflict with Druidism that it fostered disloyalty? Or was it that the Druids preserved practices of a savagery incompatible with the standards of civilisation expected by Rome in her empire?' His conclusion is an emphatic pronouncement in favour of the second alternative. In his view the Romans were actuated, not by a policy of self-interest, but by idealism in the cause of civilization.[1] In the first section of his article he refers to some recent scholars who share his view, including Kendrick himself,[2] and also to other contemporary scholars who hold that the motive for the suppression of the druids was political expediency.[3] At the close of this, the second section

[1] Professor Last had made the same claim in his earlier paper, 'The Study of the Persecutions', *Journal of Roman Studies*, vol. xxvii (1937), p. 88.

[2] Kendrick, op. cit., p. 86.

[3] This was the view of the late E. MacNeill, op. cit., pp. 71 f. Cf. also J. Vendryes, *La Religion des Celtes* (Paris, 1948), p. 294.

of his study, Professor Last cites a formidable list of passages from the Classical period referring to the features in the Gaulish religion which were felt to be objectionable in the age in which repressive measures were taken against the druids. My own view[1] is contrary to that of Professor Last, and in the present study I shall attempt to show that the active suppression of the druids has been exaggerated, but that the Romans discountenanced the druids on the ground of their subversive political influence and their extremely conservative Gaulish nationalism and anti-Roman bias. The decline of druidism was inevitable in the face of the spread of Roman culture in Gaul after the Conquest.

This difference of opinion is not merely a matter of personal interpretation of the evidence. My more serious point of difference from Professor Last is that in order to demonstrate his main thesis he has selected and presented his evidence with what seems to me to be undue emphasis on the cruel customs of the druids to the exclusion of their other functions. Assuming at the outset that the druids were priests, he identifies them with the religious practices of the Gauls in general—and more especially, those practices which were cruel and barbarous—even when no connexion with the druids is suggested in the context which he is using. He makes practically no reference to the cultural aspect of druidism, and no reference to the problem of the relationship of the druids to the other cultural classes of Gaul, and offers no serious critical textual study of the passages which he cites, often without due regard to context or to the relationship of his sources to one another. The result appears to me to be a distorted picture of the druids and of what Caesar calls their 'discipline' (*disciplina*).

It should be said at the outset that druidism must not be

[1] Here I would call attention to the judicial note by V. Duruy on the political climate in which the Roman legislative measures which affected adversely the druids of Gaul were taken. See 'La politique des empereurs romains à l'égard du druidisme', *Séances et Travaux de l'Académie des Sciences Morales et Politiques*, Institut de France, cxiii (1880), pp. 896 ff.

regarded as a static phenomenon, for it extended over several centuries. The student of druidism has to consider, for example, how far we must regard as integral to the original institutions of the druids the changes of custom as well as the disintegration which would naturally result from later cultural changes in Gaul. Moreover the evidence of our Classical authorities is of very unequal value, and of very varying degrees of independence. Quite frequently the testimony of one writer is borrowed, sometimes directly, sometimes indirectly, from a predecessor, and of course often without acknowledgement. The extent to which this has taken place is difficult to determine. It is only by an attempt to classify our evidence in the chronological order in which it was originally written that we can hope to trace the interdependence of our informants and the stemmata of their facts. Even then we are only at the beginning of our task. Perhaps the most exacting and important part of this is to determine the climate in which our sources have been written, the bias which has governed the selection of the facts recorded, the intellectual qualifications and the experience of a given author for his task, and the knowledge and beliefs current in his Age.

A marked advance in the critical study of our earliest and most important evidence from Classical sources was made in a contribution to the Royal Irish Academy in 1960 by Professor J. J. Tierney.[1] The object of his study is to reconstruct as exactly as possible the Celtic ethnography contained in the lost work of the Stoic philosopher and historian Posidonius, a Greek scholar who was born in Syria *c.* 135 B.C., and who died not later than 50 B.C. 'This can be done', says Professor Tierney, 'by studying the work of later writers, historians, geographers, ethnographers, &c., who either quote directly from Posidonius, or provide material which can be shown to derive directly or indirectly from him', and

[1] J. J. Tierney, 'The Celtic Ethnography of Posidonius', *Proceedings of the Royal Irish Academy*, vol. 60, Section C, no. 5 (Dublin, 1960).

Tierney adds this further aim which strikes the keynote of our own attempt to demonstrate the nature of our knowledge of the druids:

> 'An attempt can be made at assessing the possible bias of these writers in using their original source, and at determining their possible or probable omissions from and additions to it.'[1]

For our purpose the prime value of Tierney's study is his stress on Posidonius as the source of our information about the druids from certainly two, and very probably three, of the most important early authorities on the subject who flourished in the first century B.C., and who were in some degree contemporary with one another, namely Strabo, Diodorus Siculus, and Julius Caesar. The accounts given by these writers have so much in common that they can not be wholly independent, though there is little exact verbal agreement among them. Taken together the statements derived from Posidonius constitute a large proportion of our most authoritative information regarding one aspect of the official practices associated with the druids. By a scholarly objective comparison and analysis of the statements of our three earliest written authorities Professor Tierney has reconstructed much of the teaching of Posidonius. It should be added that while Tierney recognizes that the work of Athenaeus also contains an important element derived from the work of Posidonius, to whom he is indebted for a number of quotations on the general customs of the Gauls, the work of Athenaeus has no direct relationship to the druids, and will form no part of our present study of evidence for druidism.

Our earliest extant texts relating to the druids, then, are embodied incidentally in the work of three of these four writers mentioned above as indebted, directly or indirectly but nevertheless closely, to Posidonius. Of these, eight chapters of Diodorus Siculus (v. 25–32) are now generally

[1] Ibid., loc. cit.

recognized to have been derived from Posidonius.[1] Strabo is, as he himself admits,[2] indebted to Posidonius for some of his information on the barbarous practices of the Gauls; and his account of their human sacrifices is so close to that of Diodorus in some details, to be discussed later, that relationship in their sources seems assured. Whether Strabo's debt is to Posidonius direct, or through an intermediate source is a disputed point to which I shall return later.

Tierney does not recognize any original element in the work of our three earliest extant writers, all of whom are, in his view, dependent on Posidonius. He even brings together Strabo's attack on the Celts just referred to and the passage in Caesar's *Gallic War*, vi. 16, and regards both passages as originating in an attack on Celtic superstitions by Posidonius. Tierney in fact builds up his reconstruction of the Celtic ethnography of Posidonius on a detailed examination of the work of these four writers, the fourth being Athenaeus. Of Posidonius he claims (p. 198):

> His material on the Celts is reproduced in summary and with some changes and additions in three later Greek authors, the historian Diodorus Siculus, the geographer Strabo, and the writer of miscellanies, Athenaeus. The similar material in Caesar's *Gallic War* is taken from Posidonius without acknowledgement, and with significant and highly debatable omissions and additions. There is very little ethnographical material in later writers on the Celts which does not come from the four authors mentioned and ultimately from Posidonius.

And Tierney concludes his inquiry (p. 223):

> What may reasonably be accepted of the tradition about the Druids is problematical, and depends primarily on our view of the tendentiousness of Posidonius, and secondarily on our view of the relationship of the four secondary sources to him, particularly that of Julius Caesar.

It is noteworthy, however, that Tierney (p. 192), following

[1] See Tierney, p. 203, after Müllenhoff, *Deutsche Altertumskunde* (Berlin, 1890–1920), pp. 303 ff.

[2] *Geographia*, iv. 4. 5.

Trüdinger, holds that Posidonius was influenced by the ethnographic remains of the much earlier Greek Timaeus, and also Agatharchides, though perhaps only in method.

Tierney himself concludes (p. 224) with the suggestion that the position of the druids has been unduly magnified, the exaggeration being due to Posidonius' preoccupation with Stoic philosophy, and to Caesar's need of material for political propaganda, to emphasize the consolidation of power in the hands of the Gaulish aristocrats. Tierney also suggests that transference of characteristics from one province to another and from one intellectual class to another (e.g. from bards (Strabo), and seers (Diodorus)) has taken place in Caesar's account. Tierney regards the druids as a priesthood which did not differ essentially from the priesthood of other barbarian nations, notably the Germans, and he rejects the view expressed by Caesar, presumably following Posidonius, that the origins of this priesthood lay in Britain. Tierney suggests that on archaeological grounds the Middle Rhine or Bohemia is more probable. He concludes that the only druid personally known to any of our informants, Divitiacus, the friend of Caesar and Cicero, could not speak Latin and cannot be regarded as a source of Cicero's knowledge of druidic theory, which Tierney claims is to be regarded as 'taken from Posidonius'. Divitiacus' ignorance of Latin is perhaps not a matter of certainty (cf. p. 106 below), and Cicero's debt to Posidonius on druidic theory is hardly proven. To these various matters we shall return later.

Professor Tierney's objective analysis of the evidence and his reconstruction of the teaching of Posidonius is a work of scientific criticism, and will be the starting-point for all future work on the nature and history of the druids. Since, however, the evidence on the druids is only an incidental part of his main theme, which is the reconstruction of the lost ethnographical work of Posidonius on the Celts of Gaul, and since the evidence of Alexandrians and other later writers only enters his thesis quite incidentally, it may perhaps be desirable to give fuller consideration to some aspects of the subject, and to some later Classical writers, who lie outside his subject or are peripheral to it. In general it may be fairly concluded from his thesis that in his view all later observations on the druids, including the philosophical teaching attributed to them, are ultimately derived from Posidonius, either directly, or by inference.

Tierney's searching analysis of the history and interdependence of our sources is especially relevant to the three most disputed matters relating to the druids, viz. their status in relation to the other intellectual classes of Gaul; the relative importance of human sacrifice in what Caesar has aptly called their *disciplina*; and the nature of their intellectual activities. While we shall be inclined to modify some of Tierney's conclusions, and to take into consideration some historical developments which lie outside his main study, we shall begin our efforts to ascertain the basic elements of druidism by a close examination of his investigation of these three basic aspects of the druidic order. Only then can we hope to add some modifications which may suggest themselves by watching the developments of druidism during a number of years under changing historical conditions, and in relation to the philosophical movements in the ancient world at the period when the druids were at the height of their prestige.

II

The Ritual Functions of the Druids in the Early Classical Sources · The Tradition of Posidonius

SOME general observations on the nature of our sources are a necessary preliminary. A large body of evidence is available in Classical authorities, but it is difficult to deal with. None of it is certainly recorded by eye-witnesses. All our authors, not excluding Caesar, are now believed to be drawing in a large part from earlier written sources. These sources are, unfortunately, for the most part no longer directly available to us, and in general we know little about them on which we can rely with certainty. Moreover it was undoubtedly the bizarre, the picturesque, and the curious aspects of druidism which attracted many Classical writers to the subject. One is conscious throughout their reports that the druids were looked upon as objects of curiosity, rather than of serious interest and dignity in their own right. The picturesque and bizarre qualities are artificially heightened. Pliny's report of the ceremony of the mistletoe is a striking instance. M. L. Sjoestedt-Jonval rightly pointed out in her study of Celtic mythology that the Romans tended to force Celtic lore to a Roman pattern, and to enter barbarian territories as tourists.[1]

Before entering upon our investigations of the evidence of Classical writers as a whole, however, it will be relevant to

[1] *Dieux et héros des Celtes* (Paris, 1940), p. 22. The work has been translated into English by Myles Dillon and published under the title *Gods and heroes of the Celts* (London, 1949). For a recent study upholding the authenticity of Caesar's equation of the Gaulish with the Roman gods see J. de Vries, 'Die Interpretatio Romana der gallischen Götter' in *Indogermanica, Festschrift für Wolfgang Krause* (Heidelberg, 1960), pp. 204 ff.

our study of the origin and nature of druidism to begin with a few words about the name *druid* itself, and with some general considerations as to the areas and peoples with whom the druids are associated. An attempt must then be made to classify chronologically as briefly as possible the information about the druids which is to be found in our earliest authorities, both those still extant and others no longer available but known to have been used by extant writers. Finally we shall inquire if it is possible in any degree to gauge the motives which in ancient times have governed the selection of material by the original authors, and later by their successors, from among the ampler evidence of which they were evidently possessed.

First as to the name—the origin of the word druid (with the plural usually *druides*) is disputed.[1] Most linguists have regarded it as cognate with the Greek δρῦς, 'an oak', as indeed did the Elder Pliny.[2] On the other hand Stokes, Thurneysen, and other Celtic linguists, including Pedersen,[3] have derived the root of the word from *δρυ-, which they regard as an intensive particle, and the second element from the root **wid-* 'to know', interpreting the word *druid* as meaning 'those whose knowledge is very great'. Thurneysen returned later to the 'oak' etymology,[4] and this seems now to be the general tendency,[5] at least as regards the prefix. Opinion still differs, however, as to whether the final syllable is merely the common Celtic dental stem *-id*, or whether it may possibly be derived from the root **wid-* 'to know',[6] the derivation being

[1] For a brief discussion of the etymology and affinities of the word, see H. M. and N. K. Chadwick, *Growth of Literature* (Cambridge, 1932), vol. i, p. 611, footnote 1; cf. also J. Vendryes, *La Religion des Celtes* (Paris, 1948), p. 291. See further more recent references cited below.

[2] *Naturalis Historia* xvi. 95 249.

[3] Holger Pedersen, *Vergleichende Grammatik der keltischen Sprachen*, vol. i (Göttingen, 1909), p. 61.

[4] Thurneysen, *Zeitschr. f. celt. Philol.* xvi. 276 f. See his discussion and references (loc. cit.)

[5] It is not universally accepted, however. The derivation from **dru-wid-es*, 'the very wise' is endorsed by F. Le Roux, *Les Druides*, p. 12.

[6] It is derived in the *Geiriadur Prifysgol Cymru* (a Dictionary of the Welsh

perhaps 'those familiar with the oak'. The latter etymology seems very doubtful and an ancient popular etymology from δρῦς ('the oak') more probable (cf. p. 38 below); but on the whole I regard the origin of the word as quite obscure.[1]

It may be added that the modern Irish word *draoi* (gen. *druadh*), earlier *druí* (from earlier **druiwi*(*d*)*s*) is classed as a dental stem, having a genitive singular form *druad* and a nominative plural *druith*. The early Welsh word *derwydd*,[2] 'prophet', 'druid', is not philologically equivalent to the Gaulish Latin *druida*, Irish *druí*, but the development of the words can hardly be wholly independent, though there is no good historical evidence for the survival of druids into the historical period in Wales. The word *drý*, and its compounds (e.g. *drý-cræft*), possibly from Irish *druí*, is used widely in Anglo-Saxon in the sense of 'magician', 'sorcerer', 'wizard', and commonly translates Latin *magus*.[3]

The name, despite the difficulties of its etymology, was probably associated in actual usage from very early times with the Greek word δρῦς, 'an oak'. Maximus Tyrius, writing in the second century A.D., states that 'the Celtic image of Zeus is a lofty oak';[4] but though this recalls to our minds the Greek oak sanctuary of Dodona, it has no direct bearing on the druids of Gaul. It is not wholly impossible that the word *druid* may have originated in a nickname derived from the oakwoods with which they are associated by Pliny, in which case it would have meant something like 'backwoodsmen'.[5] We must not overlook in this connexion the name *Drunemeton* (cf. Early Irish *nemed*, 'a sanctuary'), which was the place of

Language, Cardiff, *rhan* xv, 1960), s.v. from Brythonic **do-are-uid* (*dar* = *do* + *are*), *dar* or *dor* being an intensive particle.

[1] For a fuller comment on the etymology see the 'Vocabulaire vieux-celtique' (D), *Ogam*, v (1953), p. 64, s.v. *Druis*.

[2] Corresponding to Latin *video*, etymologically indicating 'vision' in the sense of knowledge. Cf. Old Prussian *druwis*, 'belief'.

[3] See Bosworth and Toller, *Anglo-Saxon Dictionary* (and Supplement), s.v.

[4] viii. 8; cf. also p. 37 below.

[5] 'Je ne pense pas que le mot "druides" soit un sobriquet venu de la Grèce et accepté par les Gaulois', Jullian, *La Gaule*, vol. ii, p. 85, n. 1.

reunion of the Galatian judiciary council in Asia Minor;[1] and reference may also be made to other place-names containing the element *nemeton*, e.g. *Mezunemusus* (*Medionemeton*).[2] We shall refer later (pp. 36 ff. below) to the passages in which late Classical authors, especially the more rhetorical, associate the druids with sacred groves, and especially oak forests.

It must be emphasized at the outset that the Latin word *magus* as used by Latin writers is by no means necessarily identical in meaning with 'druid', whether in Classical or Irish or British texts. In speaking of the Gauls Pliny refers to 'The druids—as they call their *magi*';[3] but he nowhere states that *magi* in general are equivalent to *druids*, and this is certainly not the case, though the terms are very frequently and quite erroneously regarded as equivalent by modern writers. We must be on our guard against translating *magus* by *druid*, whether in Classical or Irish (Latin) texts. It is true that Hippolytus classes the *magi* and the *druids* together,[4] and the early Irish glosses translate the word *druí* by *magus*. But the word *magus* is commonly used by Classical writers of various types of native priests, prophets, and magicians, and the Latin writers of Ireland and the British Isles regularly use the word *magus* for people who seem to possess any kind of magical powers. Thus Adamnán, writing in the seventh century, refers to Broichán, the *nutricius* and magician of Brude mac Maelchon, as a *magus*,[5] and in the *Life of St. Patrick* by Muirchú, a work assigned to the late seventh century, Patrick's opponents, the magicians of King Laoghaire of Tara, are referred to as his *magi*. It is not until the ninth-century text known as the *Tripartite Life of St. Patrick*[6] that they are referred to as *druidae*.

[1] Strabo, xii. 5. 1.

[2] On the element *nemet-* in Celtic place-names see Christian J. Guyonvarch, *Ogam*, xii (1960), pp. 185 ff.; xiii. 157.

[3] *Druidae ita suos appellant magos. Naturalis Historia* (ed. H. Rackham, London, 1945) xvi. 95.

[4] *χρῶνται δὲ δρυΐδαι καὶ μαγείαις, Philosophumena*, I. 22.

[5] *Life of St. Columba*, ii, cap. 33.

[6] Ed. Whitley Stokes (London, 1887), vol. ii, pp. 32, 42, 50, 92, 94, &c.; also Kathleen Mulchrone, *Bethu Phátraic. The tripartite life of Patrick*, Dublin, 1939.

It is important to note at the outset that despite the fact that Strabo declares druids, *vates*,[1] and bards to have existed throughout all the Gaulish peoples (cf. pp. 17 f. below), we have no evidence for the institution of the druids among the Celts of Italy, or Spain, nor among the Galatians of Thrace or of Asia Minor, nor even among the Celts east of the Rhine. Caesar states categorically that the Teutonic peoples were entirely without them.[2] It is partly on this account that the suggestion has been made, and is widely held, that the institution is pre-Celtic, and adopted by the Celts of Gaul and Britain from the earlier peoples among whom they settled.[3] Dottin[4] and others, following Caesar (see below), held that it was created in Great Britain, and that it was transported from there to Gaul.

'The discipline (*disciplina*) of the druids', Caesar tells us, was '*thought* to have originated in Britain and to have been introduced into Gaul from there (*in Britannia reperta atque inde in Galliam translata existimatur*)', and he adds that many still come here to improve their knowledge of the system.[5] Tacitus, with reference to the events of A.D. 59, makes spectacular reference to the druids of Anglesey.[6] Pliny also had heard of the druids in Britain, but he evidently thought that they had gone to Britain from Gaul, for after referring to the proscription of the druids by the Emperor Tiberius (cf. p. 73 below) he adds the significant words: 'Why should I call to mind these matters of a profession which has now crossed the ocean and betaken itself to the void (*inane*) beyond our world?'[7]

[1] There is a valuable note on the Celtic form of the word (Irish *fáith*, Welsh *gwawd*) by C. J. Guyonvarch, in *Ogam*, xii (1960), pp. 305 ff.

[2] *Neque druides habent qui rebus divinis praesint, neque sacrificiis student.* Caesar, *Gallic War*, vi. 21. For Caesar's Commentaries the edition of A. Klotz has been used throughout, vol. i, *Commentarii Belli Gallici*, 4th ed. (Leipzig, 1962).

[3] See Sir John Rhŷs, 'Studies in Early Irish History', *Proceedings of the British Academy* (1903–4), i, 28; J. Pokorny, 'The Origin of Druidism', *Celtic Review*, v (1908–9), pp. 1 ff. and elsewhere; see especially pp. 6 ff.

[4] *Manuel pour servir à l'étude de l'antiquité celtique* (Paris, 1915), p. 365.

[5] *Gallic War*, vi. 13.

[6] *Annals*, xiv. 30.

[7] *Naturalis Historia* (edited and translated by H. Rackham, by W. H. S. Jones, and by D. E. Eichholz, London and Harvard, 1938–1962) xxx. 4.

He then continues: 'Even today Britain is still spell-bound by magic, and performs its rites with so much ritual that she might almost seem to be the source of Persian ritual (*Britannia hodieque iam adtonita celebrat tantis ceremoniis ut dedisse Persis videri possit*)'; and then after a general observation on the universality of magic throughout the world, he concludes the chapter with a whole-hearted tribute to the Romans 'who put an end to the monstrous practices by which to kill a man was a highly religious act, and even to eat him was very salubrious (*qui sustulere monstra, in quibus hominem occidere religiosissimum erat, mandi vero etiam saluberrimum*)'.[1]

Mommsen indeed held that the occupation of Britain by the Romans was largely resolved on in order to destroy druidism at its roots.[2] This is a bold assumption; but strangely enough it was accepted by the German scholar Ihm in what is one of our most authoritative modern studies of the druids,[3] and it has been endorsed by Sir Ronald Syme and R. G. Collingwood.[4] Taking the evidence together it would seem that the area of the druids was not widespread.

We will now endeavour to estimate the value of the information handed down to us from Classical authors on the nature and function of the druids. This information, though very considerable in bulk, is varied and at times irreconcilable, even contradictory. As we have said already (p. 11 above) even our earliest authors are not reporting as eye-witnesses, but are deriving their material, in a large part, from earlier written sources. We have indeed no certainty that even these earliest written sources are speaking of the druids from first-hand knowledge, though Posidonius claims some first-hand knowledge of the practices of the Gauls, including their

[1] Loc. cit.

[2] *The Provinces of the Roman Empire from Caesar to Diocletian* (transl. by W. P. Dickson, London, 1909, vol. i, pp. 105, 185). Cf. also J. B. Bury, *A History of the Roman Empire* (London, 1893), p. 257.

[3] See Pauly–Wissowa, *R.-E.*, vol. v, 2, s.v. *Druidae*, col. 1730 ff.

[4] *Cambridge Ancient History*, vol. x (Cambridge, 1934), p. 797.

head-hunting and head preservation. It is now generally recognized that Caesar's account is not based, at least wholly, on first-hand knowledge, but is derived in part from Posidonius.[1] His knowledge of the geography of Gaul as a whole is not intimate, and the information which he gives relating to this subject is very sparing, though place-names and river names are given in sufficient numbers to make clear the outline of his narrative. His indications of western Gaul are vague to the point of inaccuracy.[2]

In order to avoid repetition and to facilitate reference by placing under their relative dates our earliest Classical sources, I have prefixed to the beginning of the present work a brief chronological list of most of the Classical authors to whom reference is made in the following pages.

Beginning with the earliest extant writers, Caesar, Strabo, and Diodorus Siculus, all roughly contemporary and writing in the first century B.C., we find that of these Strabo and Diodorus are concerned to divide the intellectual classes of Gaul into three categories who were especially revered. Similarly Ammianus Marcellinus, although writing much later—in the fourth century A.D., but deriving his material from Timagenes who wrote under Augustus—divides the intellectual classes of Gaul into three classes. Caesar, however,

[1] A. Klotz, *Cäsarstudien* (Leipzig and Berlin, 1910), p. 120.

[2] On Caesar's geographical indications of Gaul see J. O. Thomson, *History of Ancient Geography* (Cambridge, 1948), p. 192. It is believed by many Classical scholars that certain passages in the *Gallic War* are interpolations. Klotz treats entire pages as geographical interpolations drawn from the works of Timagenes and introduced into the text in the early years of the Christian era (cf. his edition of *Cäsarstudien*, 1910). L.-A. Constans, while agreeing with Klotz (who, in his edition of 1952, still places brackets round iv. 10; v. 12–14; vi. 25–28) that certain geographical passages (especially i. 1. 5–7) are an interpolation in the text, claims that it is Caesar himself who has inserted into his narrative geographical extracts compiled and translated from the Greek by one of his secretaries. 'Il y a interpolation, si l'on veut, mais interpolation contemporaine de la publication de l'ouvrage, et opérée par l'auteur lui-même' (*César, Guerre des Gaules*, texte établi et traduit par L.-A. Constans (Paris, 1926), p. xiv). This question of interpolation however has little bearing on the question of Caesar's passage on the druids. It is generally agreed that the *Gallic War* as a whole is Caesar's work, and Constans himself, in estimating Caesar as a historian, concludes that 'les sources historiques de César sont bonnes' (loc. cit.).

recognizes only one class, the druids, apart from the military class.

According to Strabo[1] these three intellectual classes are (1) *βάρδοι*, 'panegyric poets', whom he defines more closely as *ὑμνηταί*, and *ποιηταί*; (2) *οὐάτεις*. These are defined as *ἱεροποιοί*, 'sacrificers' (i.e. diviners), and *φυσιολόγοι*, 'natural philosophers'; and (3) *δρυΐδαι*, who practise both *ἡ φυσιολογία*, 'natural philosophy', and *ἡ ἠθική*, 'moral philosophy'. Diodorus Siculus tells us[2] that the Gauls have (1) *ποηταὶ μελῶν* (lit. 'lyric poets') whom they call *βάρδοι*; and (2) *φιλόσοφοι*, 'philosophers' so to speak, and *θεολόγοι*, 'theologians', whom they call *Δρυΐδαι* and who are held in great veneration; and (3) *μάντεις*, 'diviners', who foretell the future by means of the flight or cries of birds and of the slaughter of sacred animals. Ammianus Marcellinus[3]—who, though writing in the second half of the fourth century, cites as his authority Timagenes, a Greek historian of Alexandria who flourished about the beginning of the first century A.D.—relates[4] that the Gauls were civilized by the *bardi*, 'bards', and the *euhages* and the *drasidae*, the latter a bad reading for *δρυΐδαι*, 'the druids'. *euhages* (var. *eubages*)[5] is almost certainly an erroneous form for the Greek *εὐαγεῖς*, a misreading of *οὐάτεις* (cf. p. 19 below), apparently the Latin *vates* (Greek *οὐάτεις*, cf. Strabo), although *vates* may have been borrowed into Latin from the Celts.[6] Klotz believed that the *οὐάτεις* of Strabo is a corruption of the postulated *εὐαγεῖς*, presumably thought by him to be from Posidonius; but this is not a suggestion to be regarded seriously.[7] It

[1] *Geographia*, iv. 4.

[2] v. 31.

[3] xv. 9. 8. For the text of Ammianus see C. U. Clark, *Ammiani Marcellini Rerum Gestarum Libri Qui Supersunt*, 2 vols. (vol. i, Berlin, 1910; vol. ii, Berlin, 1915).

[4] xv. 9. 30, 32 (*bis*).

[5] So Gelenius in his edition published at Basle in 1533. For the variant readings see the edition by Clark cited above, note ad loc.

[6] Cf. Irish *fáith*, 'a prophet', which corresponds philologically to the Latin *vatis* p, 15, n. 1 above. Zeuss first suggested that *euhages* is a bad reading for *οὐάτεις*, and his conclusion has been generally adopted. See Zeuss, *Grammatica Celtica* (2nd ed., Berlin, 1871), p. 46.

[7] *Cäsarstudien*, p. 120. Cf. K. Trüdinger, *Studien zur Geschichte der griechisch-römischen Ethnographie* (Leipzig and Berlin, 1910), p. 94, n. 1.

may be added that ancient Ireland knew all three classes, whom they call *bard*, *fili* (pl. *filid*), and *druí* (pl. *druad*), a fact which suggests strongly that the classes and their titles are ancient.

It will be seen that while Strabo, Diodorus, and Ammianus are in agreement in regard to a general threefold division into categories, and even in regard to the names of two of these categories, namely the bards and the druids, they differ in regard to the name which they apply to the third category. The οὐάτεις of Strabo would seem on the face of it to correspond to the μάντεις of Diodorus, and even to the *euhages* of Ammianus; but we shall see that there is difficulty in these identifications, owing to the fact that there is some contradiction in regard to the functions which these authors ascribe to the class in question, as well as to the druids. The contradiction is probably due to confusion in their interpretation of their sources by the authors in question. After a very full and clear analysis of our evidence Ihm[1] came to the conclusion that 'Our sources do not give us enough evidence to distinguish the relationship of the *vates* to the druids.' From this I would not readily dissent.

Having noted the three categories into which our earliest authorities (with the exception of Caesar) divide our Gaulish intellectual classes, we may now turn to consider more fully the functions of the three categories.

Strabo[2] refers (cf. p. 18 above) to the druids practising the 'interpretation of nature' (φυσιολογία), and moral philosophy (ἠθικὴ); and to the *vates* as sacrificers (ἱεροποιοί) and interpreters of nature (φυσιολόγοι). The druids, he tells us, are considered the most just of men and for this reason they are entrusted with the decision of all cases, both private and public. Formerly they even acted as arbitrators in cases of war, and forced those on the point of fighting to desist. Above all, they were entrusted with the settlement of suits for manslaughter.

[1] See Pauly–Wissowa, *R.-E.*, Vol. v, 2, s.v. *Druidae*, col. 1730 ff.

[2] *Geographia*, iv. 4.

It would seem that Strabo has here omitted (? inadvertently) a passage on divination by human sacrifice—in all probability the passage quoted below.

There follows a brief mention of the belief of the Gauls that when there are a large number of these (manslaughter) cases the harvest will be plentiful, and this is followed by a statement in a single sentence that the druids, 'and others as well', believe in the indestructibility of the human soul and the universe, although at some time fire and water will prevail over them. The entire passage, including that of the preceding threefold classification, is far from clear and reads like an abbreviated extract from some longer text. It is important therefore to bear in mind that Strabo's next chapter consists of a detailed and very interesting but emphatically censorious and contemptuous account of the Celts. In this account he includes their custom of bringing home from battle the heads of their enemies and nailing them to the entrances of their homes, and for this he cites as his authority Posidonius, 'who says that he himself saw the spectacle in many places, and that although at first he loathed it, afterwards, through his familiarity with it, he could bear it calmly'.

Strabo then continues with the well-known account of the Gaulish custom of embalming the heads of distinguished enemies and exhibiting them to strangers, declining to give them back (presumably to the relatives) for their weight in gold. At this point he observes: 'The Romans put a stop to these customs, as well as to all those connected with the sacrifices and divinations that are opposed to our usages.' He then adds a brief note on the sacrifices and divinations in question: 'They', that is to say, the Gauls, 'used to strike a man whom they had devoted to death in the back with a knife, and then divine from his death-throes; but they did not sacrifice without the druids (*ἄνευ δρυϊδῶν*).'

But surely there is some confusion in Strabo's writing. The sentence recording the belief of the Gauls that 'a big yield from these cases ensures a big yield from the land' hardly follows coherently from the brief mention of murder trials; and immediately afterwards a sentence—apparently an interpolation—refers to the indestructibility of the human soul and of the universe, which would surely come more relevantly in association with the human sacrifices.

But again a brief note is added after the statement relating the practice of divination from the death-throes of human sacrifice. 'We are told of still other kinds of sacrifices; for example they would shoot victims to death with their arrows, or impale them in temples, or, having built a *colossus* of straw and wood, throw into the *colossus* cattle and animals of all sorts and human beings, and then make a burnt offering of the whole thing.'[1]

Again the passage is somewhat incoherent, and reads like extracts in the form of notes, even interpolations perhaps added later by Strabo to his draft text. The account is almost certainly taken, like the preceding one about the Gaulish custom of preserving the heads of their enemies, from Posidonius, for the chapter (6) about the women of the Samnitae which follows immediately on our passage, opens with the words: 'In the ocean, he says'—'he' clearly a continuation of his extract from Posidonius.

The entire passage is couched in terms derogatory to the Gauls. Incidentally we may emphasize firstly that there is no hint that the victims are burnt alive, though neither is this precluded. Secondly the information is manifestly intended as a general account of sacrifices among the Gauls. There is nothing to suggest that the druids are responsible for the existence of the custom, but only that their presence is essential.[2] The only characteristic of the druids clearly defined by Strabo is that of just judges, though he also vaguely credits them with *expertise* in natural and moral philosophy. It is possible—though of course by no means certain—that

[1] Translation by H. L. Jones (London and New York, 1932).

[2] Dottin stresses the distinction (op. cit., p. 366)—rightly as it seems to me.

the presence of druids at the sacrifices was that of officials to check procedure and prevent excess or miscarriage of justice.

The passage relating to the burnt sacrifice of *colossoi* in a framework of wood and wicker closely resembles a passage in Caesar to be discussed later, and can hardly be wholly independent of it. The entire tenor of the passage is strongly anti-Gaulish and pro-Roman in sentiment, and this also we shall find to coincide with the bias of Caesar's report. Strabo's threefold classification of the intellectual categories of Gaul, however, corresponds with that of Diodorus Siculus and with that of Ammianus Marcellinus, though their functions differ somewhat. There is a definite relationship between all three passages though its precise nature is difficult to determine. On the whole, the relationship between Strabo and Diodorus is the closest, despite the discrepancy or apparent confusion in regard to the functions of the *μάντεις* and the *vates*.

Diodorus[1] tells us (cf. p. 18 above) that in addition to the bards the Gauls have 'philosophers' (*φιλόσοφοι*) and 'theologians' (*θεολόγοι*) whom they call 'druids' (*Δρυΐδαι*), and who are honoured exceedingly. And they also make use of 'seers' (*μάντεις*) who foretell the future by augury from the flight of birds and by divination from the sacrifice of victims. He then proceeds directly to report how on occasions of great moment they devote to death a human being, and after plunging a dagger into him they read the future from the manner of his fall and the twitching of his limbs and the flow of blood. And he adds that it is their custom never to make a sacrifice 'without a philosopher' (*ἄνευ φιλοσόφου*), for they say that offerings acceptable to the gods must be made through those who are acquainted with their nature, since they know their language.[2] Finally he concludes that not only

[1] v. 31.

[2] Is this possibly a reference to some formula or liturgy? If so it is unique in regard to the druids.

in peace, but also in their wars both the Gauls and even their enemies obey 'these men and their chanting poets'.[1] Even when two armies are about to open battle 'these men' (*οὗτοι*) will step between them and force them to desist as one might charm wild beasts.[2]

The passage is far from clear, but the words seem to imply that Diodorus considers that it is the *μάντεις* who are augurs and actually responsible for the sacrifice, for it is immediately after the mention of the *μάντεις* and their two kinds of augury that Diodorus enters what appears to be a parenthesis describing the nature of the form of divination by the human sacrifice. In fact his distinction between 'druids' and *μάντεις* is not clear, and the obscurity is increased by final stress on the public authority of 'these men' and their ability to prevent battle at the last moment—an authority which Strabo ascribes to the druids.

The general description of the Gauls is much fuller and more comprehensive in Diodorus than in Strabo, especially in regard to their social and military customs. Speaking of the Gauls as a whole he mentions briefly and incidentally, as Strabo does also, that the teaching of Pythagoras prevails among them to the effect that the souls of men are deathless (*ἀθανάτους*), and after a definite number of years they will enter upon a new life.[3] He gives an account of their treatment of the heads of their enemies,[4] moreover, which is strikingly close to that of Strabo, even verbally, and in both authors we note the similar though obscure phrase in regard to the compulsory presence of the druid (Strabo) or 'philosopher' (*φιλόσοφος*, Diodorus) during augury by stabbing a living

[1] This perhaps refers to the bards (*βάρδους*).

[2] *οὐ μόνον δ' ἐν ταῖς εἰρηνικαῖς χρείαις, ἀλλὰ καὶ κατὰ τοὺς πολέμους τούτοις μάλιστα πείθονται καὶ τοῖς μελῳδοῦσι ποιηταῖς, οὐ μόνον οἱ φίλοι, ἀλλὰ καὶ οἱ πολέμιοι. πολλάκις γὰρ ἐν ταῖς παρατάξεσι πλησιαζόντων ἀλλήλοις τῶν στρατοπέδων καὶ τοῖς ξίφεσιν ἀνατεταμένοις καὶ ταῖς λόγχαις προβεβλημέναις, εἰς τὸ μέσον οὗτοι προελθόντες παύουσιν αὐτούς, ὥσπερ τινὰ θηρία κατεπᾴδαντες. οὕτω καὶ παρὰ τοῖς ἀγριωτάτοις βαρβάροις ὁ θυμὸς εἴκει τῇ σοφίᾳ καὶ ὁ Ἄρης αἰδεῖται τὰς μούσας.*

[3] *συμβέβηκε καὶ δι' ἐτῶν ὡρισμένων πάλιν βιοῦν εἰς ἕτερον σῶμα τῆς ψυχῆς εἰσδυομένης* (v. 28).

[4] v. 29.

man. The closely similar descriptions occur in close juxtaposition in both authors—the definition of the threefold intellectual classes; the treatment of enemy heads; then the reference to divination and the description of the human sacrifice; the teaching of Pythagoras on the immortality of the soul. Diodorus introduces an element of obscurity by his addition of 'these men' and their part in preventing battle, as if it were an afterthought, whereas Strabo introduces it earlier, and in close connexion with the high prestige of the druids as just arbitrators. The reference to the immortality of the soul occurs earlier in Diodorus than in Strabo.

There can be no doubt that, as already stated (p. 18 above) Strabo and Diodorus are ultimately deriving their information from a common source and that, despite discrepancies, they are even following a similar text. Strabo cites Posidonius as his authority for the passage on the embalmed heads, and Posidonius is doubtless the original source of the whole passage. Strabo seems to have rearranged this original. But is the debt of Strabo and Diodorus to Posidonius direct? Or is it possibly due to an intermediary, perhaps Timagenes,[1] who is in fact cited elsewhere by Strabo?[2]

It has been argued at some length by A. Klotz[3] that Strabo's debt to Posidonius was incurred through the intervening source of Timagenes. On the other hand in a brief but important recent study Laqueur pointed out that much of Strabo's account relates to conditions later than those current in the time of Posidonius, and is stylistically characteristic of Strabo and probably his own additions to the material derived by him from Posidonius. It is unlikely, as Tierney in his recent study points out (p. 207), that these additions were made by Timagenes, partly because Strabo

[1] On Timagenes see the important article by R. H. Laqueur in Pauly–Wissowa, *R.-E.*, 2nd series, vol. vi A, 1936, cols. 1063 ff.

[2] His evidence for the sacred lake of Toulouse is cited by Strabo (iv. I. 13) side by side with that of Posidonius, though the authority of the latter is preferred. He is also cited by Strabo (xv. I. 57) as one of the authorities on the Hyperboreans, where, however, his evidence is discredited.

[3] *Cäsarstudien*. See especially pp. 69 f., 120 ff.

mentions him only once in his *Geographia*,[1] though we know that he made use of him in his *History*—partly because Strabo's references to Caesar and Augustus are those of friendship and admiration, while our scanty remains and knowledge of Timagenes would lead us to expect from him the direct opposite.[2] In fact the whole of this section of Strabo's *Geographia* is a pointed attack on the Celts, and reads like a justification of Caesar's activities against their institutions and Augustus' efforts to 'romanize' them. In further support of Strabo's direct indebtedness to Posidonius Tierney emphasizes the prominence of the number three in regard to the honourable and learned classes among the Gauls, and also that the class of the seers was very important to Posidonius. This question of a possible intermediary between Strabo and Posidonius is not, however, important for our subject, and may be left to specialists in the use made by Strabo of his sources as a whole. His close debt in some form to Posidonius is not open to doubt.

Ammianus, in common with Strabo and Diodorus, recognizes three categories whom he defines, as we have seen, as bards, *euhages*, and *drasidae*, which appear in the manuscripts in various corrupt forms, clearly derived from a Greek text. As already observed (p. 18) *drasidae* can be no other than δρυΐδαι, and the explanation first suggested by Zeuss[3] that the *euhages* of Ammianus is a corruption of the οὐάτεις, itself a transliteration of Latin *vates* (cf. Strabo), is acceptable. It is clear that Ammianus' account is not wholly independent of those of Strabo and Diodorus, but it is very brief, and there are discrepancies. Ammianus tells us that the *euhages* examined the glories of nature. Like Strabo and Diodorus, he refers to the belief in the immortality of the soul which he ascribes to Pythagoras, and attributes this doctrine to the druids.[4] After speaking of the *euhages* he

[1] iv. 1. 13.

[2] See R. H. Laqueur, loc. cit., col. 1063.

[3] *Grammatica Celtica* (loc. cit.).

[4] Strabo adds the words 'in common with others'.

continues: 'The druids, who were of a loftier intellect, and bound by the rules of brotherhood as decreed by Pythagoras' authority, were exalted by investigations of deep and serious study, and despising human affairs, declared souls to be immortal (*immortales*).'[1]

We shall return to the so-called Pythagorean doctrine later. Here also, however, it would seem likely that Ammianus is also echoing the same ultimate source as Strabo and Diodorus. Ammianus, however, refers to Timagenes a short distance before our passage, and Timagenes is evidently his more immediate source, and is doubtless favoured by Ammianus because, as an anti-Roman, he would draw a favourable picture of Gaul. In accordance with this Ammianus gives a favourable picture of the druids, making no reference to their association with human sacrifices, or to these and other discreditable practices of the Gauls as a whole.

Caesar, as we have seen, distinguishes only two classes in Gaul who are held to be of importance—one military (*equites*) and the other intellectual, to which he gives the name 'druids' (*druides*). The druids are concerned with divine matters and with the due performance of both public and private sacrifices, and the correct interpretation of ritual.[2] Their prestige as judges in all matters public and private is paramount, and their decisions are final.[3] Later, in a different context[4] he speaks of the proneness of the whole nation of the Gauls to ritual observances. Upon occasions of great danger, whether public or private, they immolate human victims, or vow to do so (*aut pro victimis homines immolant aut se immolaturos vovent*), employing the druids at the conducting of these sacrifices (*administrisque ad ea sacrificia druidibus utuntur*). He adds as a rubric that this is done because it is their belief that in order to appease the gods a life must be paid for a man's life. He continues, in words closely

[1] v. 28.

[2] Illi rebus divinis intersunt, sacrificia publica ac privata procurant, religiones interpretantur. [3] *Gallic War*, vi. 13. [4] Ibid. vi. 16.

recalling those of Strabo, that 'Others (*alii*) make use of colossal figures composed of twigs which they fill with living men and set on fire.' The victims are preferably criminals, but if the supply fails the innocent are used. Caesar refers to this practice[1] only incidentally in a brief account of the superstitions and barbaric practices of the Gauls. In general the passage corresponds closely with the accounts given by Strabo (iv. 5) and Diodorus (v. 31. 3; 32. 6), and though Caesar makes no allusion to divination in this connexion, his general account may safely be attributed to the same ultimate source as theirs.[2]

Such diversity as appears in our three authors seems to have arisen for the most part at a late stage, and to be due largely to compression and over-simplification, as well as to the personal bias of our authors. The deficiencies of Caesar's account are perhaps to be ascribed to the haste and difficulties of the circumstances in which it was written, and also to the necessity of impressing the Roman senate with the barbarism of the Gauls. It would seem that both Strabo's account—an unveiled attack upon the Gauls—and the closely related passage by Diodorus, together with Caesar's passage in the *Gallic War*, vi. 16, were inspired in the first instance by an attack on Celtic superstitions by Posidonius. We must in any case recognize that this unfavourable aspect of druidism reflected in the work of Caesar, Strabo, and Diodorus represents a policy pledged to uphold the Roman imperial attitude unsympathetic to a foreign barbaric society.

There are, however, features in Caesar's account which place it in some degree apart from those of Strabo and Diodorus. His simplification of the Gauls into two classes, the *equites* (the military class) and the *druides* ('druids') has probably no special significance. It rather suggests that under the term 'druids' he includes the intellectual classes of Gaul as a whole, and that he was either ignorant of, or indifferent to, individual distinctive functions. In addition, however, we

[1] Ibid. [2] Cf. A. Klotz, *Cäsarstudien*, p. 120.

shall see later that he adds important information about the activities of the druids not found in Strabo and Diodorus, which was not necessarily derived from Posidonius. These additions of Caesar have a weighty bearing on the importance of the druids as a potential political subversive element. Meanwhile it is interesting to observe that, as pointed out by Tierney, the position of the druids is considerably more modest in our Greek authorities, Strabo and Diodorus, than in Caesar.

Lucan also, writing in the first century A.D., refers to only two intellectual classes in Gaul, whom he refers to as bards and *dryadae*, 'druids'. The bards here as elsewhere appear to be heroic panegyric poets. The reference to the druids occurs in a passage celebrating Caesar's victories over the barbarian tribes in the West, and Lucan, like the earlier authors discussed above, is clearly concerned to uphold the Roman policy of the repression of the druids, to whom he attributes 'barbaric rites and a forbidding mode of worship in deep groves' (*barbaricos ritus moremque sinistrum sacrorum . . . nemora alta remotis incolitis lucis*).[1] There is possibly a veiled allusion here to human sacrifices though such an interpretation of the passage is certainly not essential. Lucan may, indeed, be indebted to Caesar himself, perhaps through the intermediary of the lost books of Livy, whose theme of the greatness of imperial Rome forms a dominant element in the surviving books of his *History*.

Taking these passages as a whole it appears to me that while the human sacrifice was represented in the original source as a common Gaulish custom it is not at all clear that the druids were anywhere regarded as responsible either for the actual existence of the custom, or even for its due performance. Their official presence alone is stated, and was evidently an essential feature. The custom of human sacrifice is widely attested for the Gauls as a whole. As early as *c.* 270 B.C. the poet Sopater speaks of the 'Galatians'—by

[1] *Pharsalia*, i. 447 ff.

whom Gauls may be indicated—sacrificing their prisoners to the gods by burning after a victory,[1] but there is no mention here of druids. Cicero, in his oration *Pro Fonteio*, refers to the prevalence of human sacrifice among the Gauls as to a well-known fact even in his own day (*ad hanc diem*)[2] but he makes no reference to druids in this context.

Pomponius Mela, writing in the middle of the first century A.D., corroborates the earlier statements about human sacrifices among the Gauls; but he now reports them only as a thing of the past. He describes the Gauls as proud, superstitious, and 'at one time so savage that they believed a man to be highly pleasing as a sacrifice to the gods. There still remain some traces of their former savagery in that although they abstain from actual slaying, they nevertheless cut away a fragment of their victims when they bring them to the altars.' Mela continues: 'They have, further, their eloquence and their Druids, teachers of wisdom, who profess to know the greatness and shape of the earth and the universe, and the motion of the heavens and of the stars and what is the will of the gods.'[3] No reference is made to the druids, however, as in any way connected with the sacrifices. This is the more remarkable since Mela gives an account of their teaching which bears close resemblance to Caesar's account and is indeed very probably directly indebted to it.

'They teach many things to the noblest of the race in sequestered and remote places during twenty years, whether in a cave or in secluded groves. One of their dogmas has

[1] Athenaeus, iv. 51.

[2] Cicero, *Pro Fonteio* 14 (10), 31. Cf. Dionysius of Halicarnassus, i. 38 (*καὶ παρὰ Κελτοῖς εἰς τόδε χρόνου γίνεται*).

[3] Gentes [*sc.* Galliae] superbae, superstitiosae, aliquando etiam immanes adeo, ut hominem optimam et gratissimam diis victimam crederent. Manent vestigia feritatis iam abolitae, atque ut ab ultimis caedibus temperant, ita nihilominus, ubi devotos altaribus admovere, delibant. Habent tamen et facundiam suam magistrosque sapientiae druidas. Hi terrae mundique magnitudinem et formam, motus coeli ac siderum, et quid dii velint scire profitentur (*De Chorographia, Libri Tres*, edited by Carolus Frick, Leipzig, 1880, iii. 2). I would interpret the statement from Pliny cited on p. 70 below as probably to be explained in the light of this modification noted by Mela.

become widely known so they may the more readily go to wars: namely that souls are everlasting, and that among the shades there is another life.'[1]

In fact we may safely regard it as a reasonable conclusion that the texts which survive from writers of the first century B.C., including much of the material incorporated by Caesar together with the accounts of the druids which we derive from Pomponius Mela and Lucan, are all in direct line of descent from the work of Posidonius.[2] Pomponius Mela and Lucan belong to a later period, namely the first century A.D.; but Mela's statements about the druids are even verbally so closely related to those of Caesar as to suggest direct borrowing, or at least a very close relationship.

It must be mentioned that Tacitus speaks of human sacrifices in Anglesey, but he does not associate them particularly or specifically with the druids. He merely says, speaking of Suetonius' attack on Anglesey, that the druids 'lifting up their hands to heaven, and pouring forth maledictions, awed the Roman soldiers by the unfamiliar sight'. Then later, after describing the combat, he continues: 'A force was next set up over the conquered, and their groves [i.e. of the conquered population of Anglesey], devoted to cruel superstitions, were cut down. They deemed it a duty, indeed, to cover their altars with the blood of captives, and to consult their deities through human entrails.'[3]

To this picture of the druids of Anglesey I shall return later (pp. 38, 78 below). It would be interesting to pursue here and elsewhere the question of Tacitus' probable debt to previous writers, including those cited above.

[1] Docent multa nobilissimos gentis clam et diu, vicenis annis, aut in specu aut in abditis saltibus. Unum ex his quae praecipiunt in vulgus effluxit, videlicet ut forent ad bella meliores, aeternas esse animas vitamque alteram ad manes (loc. cit.).

[2] A. Klotz, op. cit., pp. 120 f.

[3] *Annals*, xiv. 30. Praesidium posthac impositum victis excisique luci saevis superstitionibus sacri; nam cruore captivo adolere aras et hominum fibris consulere deos fas habebant.

III

The Wider Functions of the Druids in the Early Classical Sources · The Tradition of Caesar and Pliny

It is noticeable that in references to the druids by writers of the first century A.D. a new element has entered into the traditions which is not found in our earliest extant authorities. This is the deep and sequestered woods and groves with which the druids are associated. They are referred to specifically by Mela, Lucan, and, by implication, by Tacitus, and we shall see that they form a major part of the background of the druids in the account of the elder Pliny. To this subject we shall return later; but first we must examine the important account of the druids given by Pliny himself.

Pliny gives us the fullest account of the druids which dates from the first century A.D.; but the picture which we form from the scattered notices in his work differs widely from that of earlier writers. Pliny presents the druids as doctors and magicians, or a combination of the two, dealers in unnatural natural science; and he emphasizes their medical and magical practices,[1] and their possession of magical recipes.[2] It should be said, however, that in these subjects lay his special interests, and they form the theme of a large part of his enormous work, wholly independently of his few brief notices of the druids. Moreover interest in magic was in great favour in Gaul in his day, as he himself emphasizes.[3]

1 See his *Naturalis Historia* (ed. cit.), xvi. 95; xxiv. 62, 63.
2 *Nat. Hist.* xxiv. 62. Cf. Ihm in Pauly–Wissowa, *R.-E.*, s.v. *Druidae*.
3 *Nat. Hist.* xxx. 4.

This medico-magical subject, and natural or pseudo- science, accordingly form the theme of his *Naturalis Historia*, and may easily lead us to assign a disproportionate place to medicine in the importance of the druids. Tierney (p. 215) gives it as his belief that 'There can be little doubt that the medico-magical side of the Druids so prominent in Pliny's *Natural History* is the real historical basis of their power and influence, and that the rest is a mere ideological superstructure.' But it may be pointed out that, important as Pliny's testimony is to the medical and magical practices of the druids, this testimony is relatively late, and none of our other authorities, either earlier or later, lays any stress on them, with the possible exception of the statement of Suetonius about the 'serpent's egg', regarded as a symbol of druidism, to which we shall refer later (pp. 73 f. below).

Pliny's preoccupation with medicine is quite in accordance with what we know of Gaulish traditional practice, and Pliny himself must have had a ready audience. He tells us of a number of eminent physicians in the early part of the first century B.C., who were either natives of, or who had received their training in, Gaul. Such was Crinias of Marseilles (*Massilia*) who combined astronomy with his medical practice, and who died a wealthy man, even after expending large sums on building the walls of Marseilles and other towns.[1] Pliny also speaks of Charmis, a contemporary of Crinias, also of Marseilles, who was somewhat of an innovator in the beneficial use of cold water in medical practice.[2] Martial refers to the surgeon Alcon, who was famous in Rome under Claudius, and who rapidly became very wealthy after his exile in Gaul.[3] Indeed Gaulish physicians, like Gaulish eloquence, were pre-eminent about the beginning of the Christian era and shortly before. One passage by Dio Chrysostom seems to be inspired by an animus against Gaulish orators and medicine alike.[4]

[1] *Nat. Hist.* xxix. 5.
[2] Ibid., loc. cit.
[3] xi. 84. 5.
[4] *Oratio* xxxiii, pp. 2 ff.

We have said nothing of the sources of Pliny's information, and in general they are relatively little known. It has been suggested with little probability that he may have been indebted to Cicero who was personally acquainted with the druid Divitiacus (cf. p. 109 below), and who refers in his own treatise 'On Divination' (*De Divinatione*) to the claim of Divitiacus to have been versed in natural philosophy (φυσιολογία) and augury.[1] Cicero also makes reference to a treatise in five books by Posidonius,[2] whom here and elsewhere he refers to familiarly as 'noster', and once as *nostrum familiarem*,[3] indicating a close and valued acquaintance. He states further that he had often seen and heard him in Rhodes,[4] and names him as his fourth teacher.[5] He made use of Posidonius' writings in both his *De Natura Deorum* ii, and *De Divinatione* i. It is not altogether impossible therefore that Pliny may also have been indebted to Posidonius for some of the medico-magical lore with which he credits the druids; but this is highly improbable. And the political attitude of Pliny to the druids and the benefit conferred by the Romans in suppressing them are categorically expressed by himself[6] (cf. p. 73 below).

Pliny frequently cites Timaeus as his source, e.g. for his name of Sardinia (iii. 7), his reference to an island off 'Scythia' (iv. 13); another called Mictis, a source of tin to which the Britons obtain access in curraghs (iv. 16); to another called Aphrodisias (iv. 22); to the source of the Nile (v. 10)—where he is referred to as 'Timaeus the Mathematician'); to the nature and source of amber (xxxvii. 11). From this it is clear that Pliny was familiar with a fairly wide range of the works of Timaeus; but there is no suggestion that he was indebted to Timaeus for his magical or medical lore, or even for his most famous passage on the mistletoe, to

1 *De Divinatione*, i. 41, 90.
2 Ibid. i. 3. 6.
3 *De Finibus Bonorum et Malorum*, i. 2.
4 *Tusculanae Disputationes*, ii. 25, 61; cf. *Ad Atticum*, ii. 1. 'At Rhodes he studied under . . . the philosopher Posidonius' (Plutarch, *Cicero*, 4. Cf. Cicero, *Brutus*, 91).
5 *De Natura Deorum*, i. 3.
6 *Nat. Hist.* xxx. 4.

which I shall refer later. It may, indeed, be said here in anticipation that it is not easy to point to any single passage bearing directly on the druids in the work of any later authors which can be directly traced to the writings of Timaeus, though this does not preclude the possibility of some early contribution to the subject having been made by him.

The forest formed an important element in certain druidic ceremonies as reported by Pliny:

> The druids [he tells us]—for so they call their *magi*—hold nothing more sacred than the mistletoe and the tree on which it grows provided that it is a *robur*. They choose the *robur* to form oak groves, and they do not perform any religious rites without its foliage, so that it can be seen that the druids are so called from the Greek word.
>
> 'Nihil habent Druidae (ita suos appellant magos) visco et arbore, in qua gignatur, si modo sit robur, sacratius. Iam per se roborum eligunt lucos nec ulla sacra sine earum fronde conficiunt.'[1]

With this passage we may compare the note by the Scholiast to Lucan cited below (p. 36).

Pliny continues his passage about the oak (*robur*) as follows:

> Anything growing on those trees (*quidquid adgnascatur illis*) they regard as sent from heaven and a sign that this tree has been chosen by God himself. It [i.e. ? the mistletoe] is however very rarely found, and when found it is gathered with great ceremony and especially on the sixth day of the moon. . . . They prepare a ritual sacrifice and feast under the tree, and lead up two white bulls whose horns are bound for the first time on this occasion. A priest (*sacerdos*) attired in a white vestment ascends the tree and with a golden pruning-hook cuts it [? the mistletoe] which is caught in a white cloth. Then next they sacrifice the victims (*victimas immolant*) praying that God will make his gift propitious to those to whom he has given it. They believe that if given in drink it [? mistletoe] will give fecundity to any barren animal, and that it is sovereign against all poisons.[1]

This picturesque fantasia is almost the only account of the druids that is at all widely known today. It ranks with the

[1] *Nat. Hist.* xvi. 95.

stories of King Alfred and the cakes, of Cnut and the waves, and of Bruce and the spider among the classics of universal popular knowledge. The rhetorical nature of the passage, and of the other passages cited above, in which Pliny refers to the druids, taken together with the uncritical nature of Pliny's writing generally, should make us hesitate to attach too grave a credence to the passage of the mistletoe in association with the druids. If the ceremony was really important or at all widely practised it is indeed strange that we hear no hint of it from any other source. The ceremony itself would not be incompatible, however, with druidism as a forest cult. It is tempting to follow a clue suggested by two of Pliny's references to (Alexander Cornelius) Polyhistor. In one of these (xiii. 22) he cites Polyhistor as an authority on oak-trees and mistletoe and some of their characteristic features, and in another (xvi. 6) he cites him as an authority on various species of acorns. These references, however, have nothing to offer which suggests any connexion with Pliny's remarkable ceremony, and have no relevance except to indicate that Polyhistor's writing contained passages relating to various kinds of oak (including the *robur*) and mistletoe, and that Pliny knew of this.

We may now ask the question: 'What is the nature of the association of the druids with a forest cult?' Since our early sources—Caesar, Strabo, and Diodorus—make no reference to it, it probably formed no part of the report of Posidonius. It is also absent from the Alexandrian tradition to be discussed later. It is not easy, therefore, to be sure how far the forest is itself an original feature of the background of druidism. To what extent is it due to the discouragement under which the druids continued to exist from the time of Augustus onwards, as a result of which the forests may well have formed the refuge and stronghold of their later years? Apart from the possible derivation of the name (cf. pp. 12 f. above) the association of the druids with the forest does not appear to be very early, nor incidentally to be present in the Irish tradition.

Lucan refers to the druids as dwelling in deep groves and sequestered uninhabited woods, and as there practising barbarous rites and a sinister mode of worship.[1] To this passage the Scholiast adds (450): 'Et vos barbaricos ritus Driades. Moremque sinistrum contrarium nostro'; and again (451): 'Sacrorum Driadae sine templis colebant deos in silvis' (They attend upon the gods in woods without making use of temples).[2]

There is, however, a certain ambiguity here as to whether the Scholiast is making a specific reference to the druids of Gaul, or whether he is distinguishing them from, or identifying them with, a similar class among the Germani. He adds as a further comment to the above gloss: 'Driadae gens Germaniae'; and further: 'Sunt autem Driadae philosophi Gallorum dicti ab arboribus quod semotos lucos incolant; hi dicunt redire animas in alium orbem', &c. We may possibly compare the commentary of Lactantius Placidus on the *Thebais* of Statius (see below): 'The Dryads [*sic*] are those who delight in oaks' (*Dryades sunt quae quercibus delectantur*).[3] Lucan's reference in the *Pharsalia* to sacred woods, cited above, recalls the later passage in the same poem where he refers to a sacred wood near Marseilles, containing trunks of trees crudely sculptured to represent gods (*simulacra maesta deorum*),[4] where the worship of the gods is conducted with

[1] 'Et vos barbaricos ritus moremque sinistrum / sacrorum, Dryadae, positis repetistis ab armis / . . . nemora alta remotis / incolitis lucis' (*Pharsalia*, i. 450 ff.).

[2] H. Usener, *Scholia in Lucani Bellum Civile* (Leipzig, 1869), p. 33. The manuscript date of the *Scholia* is ninth century. See Zwicker, *Fontes* I, p. 49: *Lucani Commenta Bernensia*.

[3] R. Jahnke, *Lactantii Placidi qui dicitur Commentarius in Statii Thebaida* (Leipzig, 1898), p. 210.

[4] With this reference to 'effigies' of the gods we may compare the reference of Valerius Flaccus to the *Jovis simulacra* (p. 37 below) in the form of a lofty oak, and to the wooden sculpture of the early Celts, especially the herms. See P. Lambrechts, *Contributions à l'étude des divinités celtiques* (Brugge, 1942), pp. 55, 93 f. On 7 October 1963 a notice appeared on p. 9 of *The Times* of about 140 pieces of wood-carving dated from the second century A.D., and including twenty complete statues of varying size and twenty-five miniature heads. All are carved in oak, and were found in the marshland sources of the Seine, in the neighbourhood of what is believed to have been a Gallo-Roman sanctuary. Three of these wooden statues are pictured in *The Times* on p. 8.

'barbaric rites (*barbara ritu sacra deorum*), the altars heaped with hideous offerings, and every tree sprinkled with human gore'.[1] In fact, however, no human sacrifices are specifically mentioned in the former passage, and no druids in the latter. The priest attending the *dominus loci* is referred to as a *sacerdos*. With the reference to the trunks of trees sculptured to represent gods, we may perhaps compare the passage in the *Argonautica* of Valerius Flaccus[2] where reference is made to 'broken columns, effigies of Jove' (*truncae Jovis simulacra columnae*); perhaps also the passage from Statius cited below.

With the sacred wood described by Lucan we inevitably recall the wood sacred to Latonia (*nemori Latonia cultrix*) in the *Thebais* of Statius,[3] 'dense and ancient, untouched by human hand and impervious to the beams of the sun. Here the pale and uncertain light serves only to increase the awe and the ominous silence. The divine presence of Latonia haunts the grove, and the wood in its sacred shadows hides her effigies[4] in the cedar and oak.'

Lucan's wood near Marseilles then has no specific connexions with druids, and is in charge of a priest. It is as eerie as a wood in a fairy tale. 'The people never frequented the place to worship very near it, but left it to the gods. . . . The priest (*sacerdos*) himself dreads the approach and fears to come upon the lord of the grove.'[5]

In any case Lucan's obscure passage describing the wood near Marseilles cannot be taken literally as evidence,[6] nor did Lucan intend that it should be. The passage is splendid rhetoric—folklore never achieved loftier expression. The

[1] *Pharsalia*, iii. 399 ff.

[2] vi. 91. The editor states in a note to the passage that the 'broken columns must be *herms*, short pillars with an effigy at the top'. See *Valerius Flaccus*, edited and translated by J. H. Mozley (London and Harvard, 1934), p. 307, n. 1. Cf. however S. Reinach, *Revue celtique*, xiii, p. 191; and earlier P. Lambrechts, op. cit., pp. 54 f., 93; cf. also p. 36, note 4, above.

[3] *Thebais*, iv. 419 ff.

[4] Cf. p. 36 above and the references there cited.

[5] *Pharsalia*, iii. 422 ff.

[6] On this matter we may compare J. D. Duff, *Lucan* (London and New York, 1928), p. xi.

water which fell in abundance from dark springs, the coverts where wild beasts would not lie down, the motionless wood—this is the stuff of Grendel's lair in the Anglo-Saxon epic of *Beowulf*, or of the magic coverts near the spring of Berenton in the forest of Brocéliande in medieval Arthurian tradition, rather than of the haunt of a highly intellectual and politically respected class.

We have seen also (p. 30 above) that Tacitus refers to groves on the island of Anglesey which had been devoted to barbarous superstitions and which he tells us were destroyed by Suetonius Paulinus before A.D. 61 on his conquest of the island. It should be noted, however, that these references are all relatively late. The passage from Tacitus is commonly cited as evidence for the existence of groves on Anglesey in early times. Yet the conquest of Anglesey by Suetonius took place before Tacitus was adult, and it is by no means impossible that Tacitus is working up a grand rhetorical effect on some picturesque hints which he had received as oral tradition. We shall return to this later (cf. pp. 78 f. below). It is in fact not outside possibility that the entire association with oak-groves is a myth originating in early etymological attempts to indicate the origin of the name from the Greek word δρῦς, 'an oak', an etymology which, as we have seen (p. 34 above) Pliny himself endorsed.

It has been suggested[1] with much probability that the priest (*sacerdos*) referred to by Lucan in the sacred wood near Marseilles may be a *gutuater* rather than a druid. The word *gutuater*[2] is itself obscure. The word has been interpreted as 'father of voice', or of 'inspiration', and the suggestion has been made that this is the true title of a sanctuary priest, though the etymology of the word would seem rather to suggest prophetic associations. J. Loth translates the *gutuatri*

[1] Dottin, op. cit., p. 365.

[2] For the etymology see A. Holder, *Altkeltischer Sprachschatz* (Leipzig, 1896), s.v. Cf. also Dottin, op. cit., p. 82. For a recent note and comprehensive summary of references to previous suggestions see the serial 'Vocabulaire vieux-celtique', s.v. *G*, published in *Ogam*, viii (1956), p. 350.

(pl.) as 'masters of voice' (cf. Irish *guth*, 'voice'), and Pokorny suggests that the *gutuatri* (sing. *gutuater*) were the members of the Celtic clergy who had preceded the order of the druids; but evidence of their antiquity and status is wholly lacking. All we know is that they were still in existence in the Roman period.[1]

Dottin[2] held with great probability that the *gutuater* was a priest, and as such distinct from a druid; and the actual word possibly suggests a connexion with the μάντεις rather than the druids. The occurrence of the word is attested on four Gaulish inscriptions.[3] These inscriptions refer to a *gutuater* of Mars on an inscription, now lost, at Maçon (Saône-et-Loire);[4] the second inscription commemorates a *gutuater praefectus coloniae* at Le Puy-en-Valais, Haute-Loire,[5] and two inscriptions at Autun are by *gutuatri* who made dedications in honour of a local god Anvallus.[6] These inscriptions[7] in which the word *gutuater* occurs all relate to officials who appear to have been much romanized both in name and functions, whatever their relations to local gods may have been. Vendryes suggests[8] that the function of the *gutuater* may be equivalent to the role of the *antistites templi* to whom Livy refers[9] among the Boii of Italy, or to that of the *aedituus Beleni* mentioned by Ausonius.[10] The word *gutuater* (or *guturvatus*—the reading is uncertain—seems to occur probably also in a corrupt form, in Book viii of Caesar's *Gallic War*, added by Hirtius, where it is given as the name of a man of the Carnutes who, together with a certain Conetudunus, was responsible for the Gaulish revolt of 52 B.C.[11] It may here be merely a title. He must have been a person of great importance, and the part which he plays would certainly be in

1 Cf. Le Roux, *Les Druides*, p. 16.
2 Op. cit., pp. 82, 365.
3 For a recent discussion and the texts see *Ogam*, viii. 350; cf. also for details and some discussion of the inscriptions Kendrick, *The Druids*, p. 135, and the references there cited.
4 *Corpus Inscriptionum Latinarum*, vol. xiii, no. 2585, cf. 1577.
5 *C.I.L.* xiii. 1577.
6 *C.I.L.* xiii. 11225; 11226.
7 For the text of the inscriptions see *Ogam*, loc. cit.
8 *La Religion des Celtes* (Paris, 1948), p. 305.
9 xxiii. 24. 12.
10 *Professores*, x. 3.
11 *Gallic War*, vii. 3; viii. 38.

accordance with our evidence of the druids as upholders of Gaulish nationalism and anti-Roman feeling.

We have now discussed, without attempting to offer any final solution, the classification of the intellectual categories of Gaul, and the function of the druids in relation to augury and public sacrifices, including human sacrifices, as these are reported to us in our earliest surviving texts. We have called attention to the element of the forest in their cult as this appears in the reports of the first century A.D. We may now proceed to consider some of the more general characteristics of the druids, again following our informants with some attention to their chronology. For these general characteristics our earliest and fullest authority is Caesar, to whom we now return.

Despite the fact that Caesar mentions druids alone as constituting the intellectual class of Gaul, we have seen that much of what he reports of them bears a close resemblance to our information from other writers, and that in this he is probably relying on written sources which are directly or indirectly identical with theirs. To this inherited information he may have added something from his own experience in Gaul, but most probably from report only. The general result is somewhat incoherent, possibly due to the circumstances in which Caesar's *Gallic War* was composed, and possibly in some degree to over-simplification, perhaps even mistranslation,[1] of material borrowed, without acknowledgement, from Posidonius (cf. p. 8 above). We have to bear in mind the difficult conditions in which Caesar's reports may have been drawn up during his campaigns, and the political necessity of couching his reports in a form which would be calculated to meet with the approbation of the Roman senate.[2] Whatever his source, Caesar's information is important, and in some

[1] Cf. A. Klotz, *Cäsarstudien*, pp. 26 f.; de Vries, *Kairos*, ii. 67.

[2] For references to various views as to the circumstances of the composition and publication of the *Gallic War*, see P. Fabre, 'Vingt années d'études sur César' in J. Marouzeau, *Mémorial des études latines* (Paris, 1943), pp. 215 ff., especially pp. 226 f.

degree unique, and with the above considerations in mind we will follow what he tells us, supplemented (? and modified) by information from other writers.

First in regard to their organization. The druids, he tells us, formed an institution, presided over by an archdruid, who exercised supreme authority over them.[1] On his death he is succeeded by the one who holds the highest dignity (*qui summam inter eos habet auctoritatem*) and if several competitors have equal title the successor is elected by the votes of the druids. Sometimes they even dispute this dignity by arms. They do not seem to have formed a special caste, for we shall see that the druid Divitiacus was drawn from the nobility of the Aedui; but they were a privileged class, and were exempt from taxation and usually took no part in warfare.[2] Contrary to the opinion expressed by Pliny (cf. p. 15 above) Caesar states that it was believed[3] (*existimatur*) that the institution (*disciplina*) had originated in Britain, and he states that many still went there in order to acquire a more perfect knowledge of the system.[4]

In Gaul a general assembly of the druids was held at an appointed day in the year in the territory of the Carnutes 'in the centre of all Gaul',[5] probably in the neighbourhood of the modern Chartres.[6] There they held sessions on a consecrated

[1] *Gallic War*, vi. 13.

[2] Ibid. vi. 14. Druides a bello abesse consuerunt neque tributa una cum reliquis pendunt; [militiae vacationem omniumque rerum habent immunitatem]. Klotz (ed. cit.) suggests that the phrase in brackets should be deleted.

[3] Caesar is careful to report this as supposition, not as fact. This is often overlooked by modern scholars, with serious distortion of their inferences in consequence.

[4] Caesar, *Gallic War*, vi. 13. Sir John Rhŷs held that it was to Ireland rather than Britain that the druids went to learn their art, and that Caesar was misinformed. Apart from Anglesey we have no evidence of druidism in southern Britain at this period, and Rhŷs was under the impression that Anglesey was not Brythonic in the first century A.D. See his paper 'Studies in Early Irish History', *Proceedings of the British Academy* (1903–4), i. 55.

[5] Caesar, loc. cit.

[6] For a discussion of the situation and its advantages for such a union, see Jullian, *La Gaule*, ii. 97 f., and footnotes; and more recently de Vries, *Kairos*, ii. 73. De Vries suggests that 'the centre of Gaul' does not denote a point of locality, but a spiritual centre, 'eine sakrale Mitte', and that Caesar, like modern scholars, has misinterpreted it in a geographical sense.

spot. 'Hither', says Caesar, 'those who have disputes bring them from all parts and submit them to the druids for arbitration.' We are reminded of the importance of the function of judges attributed to them by Strabo (cf. p. 21 above). F. Lot points out that this assembly implies a kind of idea of unity, both judiciary and political, among the Gauls, and he compares the function of the temple of Delphi among the Greeks. 'Les Gaulois avaient donc un sentiment de celticité comme les Grecs d'hellénisme. . . . Les Romains ne s'y trompèrent pas, et l'abolition des sacrifices humaines fut un prétexte pour excuser la persécution qu'ils menèrent contre le druidisme.'[1] In a further striking passage closely corresponding with that of Strabo Caesar emphasizes the importance of the function of the druids as judges.[2] He tells us that they act as arbitrators in peace and war, and that they are the sole judges of all suits, public and private, including cases of manslaughter. The decisions, which included the assessment of the punishments, were entirely in their hands. They could enforce their sentences by excommunication which was equivalent to outlawry.

The druids were not unlettered. It is stated by Caesar that they made use of the Greek alphabet[3] for almost all other matters and for public and private affairs, yet they would not commit their learning to writing.[4] Origen also, writing in the third century A.D., comments on the absence of any known survivals of their writings.[5] Caesar himself attributes

[1] F. Lot, *La Gaule* (Paris, 1947), pp. 79 f. [2] Loc. cit.

[3] For further evidence of the use of the Greek alphabet for official purposes among certain Gaulish tribes, see J. Filip, *Celtic Civilization and its Heritage* (Prague, 1960, English translation by R. F. Samsour, 1962), p. 82.

[4] On the extent and character of the introduction of Greek culture into Gaul through the Greek colony of Marseilles, see W. von Wartburg, 'Die griechische Kolonisation in Süd-Gallien und ihre sprachlichen Zeugen im Westromanischen', *Von Sprache und Mensch* (Bern, 1956), pp. 61 ff. See further, however, R. Lautier, 'Recherche archéologique 1940, 1941, 1942', *Gallia*, ii (1943), p. 245.

[5] Ἀλλὰ καὶ τοὺς μὲν Ὁμήρου Γαλακτοφάγους, καὶ τοὺς Γαλατῶν Δρυΐδας, καὶ τοὺς Γέτας, σοφώτατα λέγει ἔθνη εἶναι καὶ ἀρχαῖα, περὶ τῶν συγγενῶν τοῖς Ἰουδαϊκοῖς λόγοις διαλαμβάνοντας, ὧν οὐκ οἶδα εἰ φέρεται συγγράμματα (*Contra Celsum*, i. 16).

the reluctance to make use of writing for literary purposes, partly to a desire that their teaching may remain esoteric—not a rare motive among early native learned classes[1]—partly to a desire that the excellently trained memories which the form necessitates may not deteriorate. This motive, however, must be estimated as Caesar's conjecture.

Caesar alone among our earliest informants emphasizes the métier of the druids as instructors.[2] He makes three references to this, and if one unpicks his text one forms a suspicion that he is here closely following previous written texts, though this is not necessarily the case, for there is no discrepancy, and he may merely be jotting down somewhat disjointed notes. First at the opening of his account, after his brief statement as to the concern of the druids in the public and private sacrifices, and in interpreting matters of religion (*religiones*), he continues: 'a large number of young men resort to them for the *disciplina*, by whom they are held in great honour.'

In the following chapter (14), after the opening statement of the exemption of the druids from military and civil obligations (cf. p. 41 above), Caesar observes that, 'Induced by such advantages (*tantis excitati praemiis*) many adopt this "discipline" of their own accord and are sent by their parents and relatives. There they are said to learn by heart a great number of verses. Some remain in the *disciplina* in this way for twenty years.' It should be noted that Caesar does not actually state specifically that the youths are the young 'nobility' of the Gauls, though this is likely enough; nor does he state that the 'twenty years' are necessarily spent in 'learning' either the *disciplina* or the great number of verses. The passage is commonly mistranslated and misunderstood in this respect. The verbs are all simple and the statements laconic: *mittuntur* (*a parentibus*, &c.); *magnum ibi numerum versuum ediscere dicuntur; itaque annos nonnulli vicenos in disciplina permanent.*

In yet a third passage later in the same chapter, after

[1] See de Vries, *Kairos*, ii. 70. [2] *Gallic War*, vi. 13.

stating his views on the reason for teaching orally, he adds that the druids 'lecture (*disputant*) and impart (*tradunt*) to the youths (*iuventuti*) many things, concerning the stars and their motion, the extent of the world and of our earth, and the "nature of things" (*natura rerum*), and the limitless power and majesty of the immortal gods'. Unfortunately none of the verses in which their oral teaching is said by Caesar to have been imparted is known to have survived, and we have no direct testimony as to its character or form. A single triad attributed to the Gymnosophists[1] and the druids by Diogenes Laertius[2] suggests that the form of the triad, this favourite Celtic convention of Irish and Welsh literature, goes back to early times: 'to honour the gods, to do no evil, and to practise bravery'.[3]

I cannot agree with those modern scholars who believe that the oral method employed by the druids in their teaching was intended to endue the lessons with exceptional solemnity, or to give them 'le prestige de puissants mystères'.[4] This seems to me to view the procedure through Hellenistic spectacles. Moreover oral teaching was the custom in the ancient world, in Athens in the centuries before the Christian era, and in the schools of Alexandria in the early centuries A.D. It is universal everywhere among early and backward peoples, such as the continental Gauls before writing became general with the conversion to Christianity, and among the Brahmins of India. It is moreover inevitable that among a people who had developed oral tradition to a high art the accomplishment would not be given up lightly for the more laborious and expensive process of writing.

Neither Strabo nor Diodorus mentions the culture or education imparted by the druids to the young Gauls, though in fact φιλόσοφοι, φιλοσοφία in Strabo and Diodorus may well imply teaching in some form. 'What is a philosopher, but

[1] The name by which the Greeks referred to certain ancient Hindu ascetic philosophers. [2] *Lives of the Philosophers*, i, Prologue, 6.

[3] σέβειν θεοὺς καὶ μηδὲν κακὸν δρᾶν καὶ ἀνδρείαν ἀσκεῖν.

[4] Jullian, op. cit. ii, 106 f.

humani generis paedagogus?' asks Seneca.[1] It would seem probable that this information was not given by Posidonius, but in the following century Pomponius Mela[2] relates that 'They teach many things to the noblest of the race in sequestered and remote places during twenty years, whether in a cave or in secluded groves' (cf. p. 29 above).

Mela's statement can hardly be independent of that of Caesar quoted above and is probably derived from the same source. It is not identical, however, for the secrecy is here referred to for the first time. It is probably a new element which entered druidical practice for the first time under Roman cultural influence, and later under direct Roman legislation, as we shall see.

In view of the importance and influence claimed by Caesar for the druids as teachers of the young, it is perhaps permissible to stress the negative side of their teaching—the almost complete absence of any clear indication which might lead us to suppose that morality or ethics—in the modern sense of the term—held any place in their system. Hence the absence of any suggestion of rewards or punishments hereafter. There is a total absence of any idea of Hell. Their teaching is nowhere reported in a way which suggests that it inculcated religion in a spiritual sense. All that one reads of their teaching as distinct from their activities would suggest that they were philosophers rather than priests[3]—whether we think of natural philosophy such as that of the early Ionians; or empirical, such as medicine and magic; but certainly not religion or ritual.

In fact the part assigned to the druids in religious ceremonies is far from clear; but it does not appear to have been prominent, or to suggest that the druids held the function of

[1] *Epistulae morales*, 89. 13. He is arguing against the view of the Stoic Aristo who did not include practical advice as any part of ethics: 'Et paedagogi esse dixit non philosophi, tamquam quidquam aliud sit sapiens quam humani generis paedagogus.'

[2] *De Chorographia*, iii. 19.

[3] Dottin is surely right in distinguishing the druids from the priestly class. See *L'Antiquité celtique*, p. 364. So also F. Lot, *La Gaule*, p. 76.

priests. We hear nothing from early writers of the local sanctuaries of native Gaulish religion, in which forests, rivers, springs, and lakes are prominent.[1] Nor do we have references to druids in relation to the Gaulish temples, altars, or images. Apart from the passage in Pliny quoted above (p. 34) we hear nothing which might suggest that they acted in the capacity of priests at religious ceremonials; nothing of liturgy, hymns, or prayers. Caesar tells us that they are concerned with divine matters, and with public and private sacrifices and that they interpreted religious matters—whatever the precise meaning of this;[2] but it is not clear that this means anything more than the practice of divination referred to by Strabo and Diodorus (cf. pp. 20, 22 above).

Of the purely secular learning of the druids we are told little and its precise nature is not always clear. How far can a distinction be drawn between prophecy and political propaganda? The two latter are closely united, especially in the later period. How far, for example, can we regard as an example of their prophetic power the announcement of the Gaulish druids in the time of Vespasian, referred to by Tacitus, that the burning of the Capitol presaged the approaching destruction of the Roman Empire and the domination of the world by the 'tribes beyond the Alps'? 'Thus the druids declaimed in their chantings of vain superstition' (*superstitione vana Druidae canebant*).[3]

Again it is not always by any means clear how far a distinction is made by our authorities between history, cosmogony, and antiquarian speculation. Caesar's statement that the Gauls declare that they are all descended from the

[1] The fact is widely attested in Classical texts. For some recent references see Vendryes, op. cit., pp. 275 ff., 279 f.; J. de Vries, *Keltische Religion* (Stuttgart, 1961), pp. 115 f., 183.

[2] Illi rebus divinis intersunt, sacrificia publica ac privata procurant, religiones interpretantur (*Gallic War*, vi. 13). Caesar nowhere uses the word *sacerdotes* of the druids. The use of the word in vii. 33 does not necessarily, or even probably, refer to druids. For the *religiones* cf. p. 110 below.

[3] Tacitus, *Histories*, iv. 54. The whole of this chapter by Tacitus is of great significance for the political anti-Roman activities of the druids.

ancestor Dis (*Dispater*), affirming that this is the assertion of the druids[1] is certainly to be classed, not as history, but as antiquarian speculation or cosmogony. On the other hand Ammianus Marcellinus implies that the druids were in fact authorities on the history of the Gauls, for 'they affirm that one portion of the Gaulish race was indigenous in Gaul, but that others had penetrated from the outlying islands and from the regions beyond the Rhine'.[2] And this information he has gathered from Timagenes[3] (cf. p. 18 above).

The gift of prophecy sometimes attributed to the druids is closely connected with augury, to which we have seen allusions in our earliest authorities. Cicero relates that his friend the famous druid Divitiacus had informed him that he used to foretell the future by observation of augury as well as 'by inference'.[4] Dio Chrysostom, writing about the beginning of the second century A.D., but probably on earlier authority, echoes the traditions of the druids as versed in the prophetic art and in wisdom in general.[5] Hippolytus, in the early third century, again refers to them as seers, prophets, and magicians.[6] The same writer observes that they are said to have foretold the future by ciphers and numbers 'after the manner of the Pythagoreans'.[7] They may have predicted after eating acorns.[8] These late Greek statements are derived from earlier writers; but it is interesting to note that they appear to be wholly unaware of traditions of the druids being present at the human sacrifices as an element in augury, as these appear in what we may now call the Posidonian tradition.

[1] Galli se omnes ab Dite patre prognatos praedicant idque ab Druidibus proditum dicunt (vi. 18). [2] xv. 9. 4. [3] Loc. cit.

[4] Qui et naturae rationem quam φυσιολογίαν Graeci appellant, notam esse sibi profitebatur et partim auguriis, partim coniectura quae essent futura dicebat (cf. p. 109 below).

[5] *Oratio* xlix. 8: Κελτοὶ δὲ οὓς ὀνομάζουσι Δρυΐδας, καὶ τούτους περὶ μαντικὴν ὄντας καὶ τὴν ἄλλην σοφίαν.

[6] *Philosophumena*, I. 22: τούτους Κελτοὶ ὡς προφήτας καὶ προγνωστικοὺς δοξάζουσιν . . . χρῶνται δὲ δρυΐδαι καὶ μαγείαις.

[7] Ibid., loc. cit. [8] Usener, *Scholia in Lucani Bellum Civile*, p. 33.

We have very little direct knowledge of the druids in either their public or their private life. Except for the famous passage of the mistletoe in Pliny we never see them in action. This is a natural result of the fact that there is no evidence that any of our informants ever met a druid or were direct witnesses of their official practices or their private life. There is, however, one notable exception. Both Caesar and Cicero were evidently familiar with Divitiacus, whom Cicero states categorically to have been a druid. Caesar does not mention the fact though he knew him intimately. Cicero mentions that Divitiacus had told him that he was familiar with the art of natural philosophy and that he used to predict the future by augury (cf. p. 109 below) but he gives no further details,[1] and Caesar refers to him only in his political capacity, as a chief of the Aedui and elder brother of Dumnorix, their ruling king, and as a leader among the Gaulish princes who supported Caesar in resisting Ariovistus and the invading Teutons. After the conquest of the Aedui by the Sequani, supported by Ariovistus, Divitiacus had made a personal journey to Rome to appeal to the senate for help. In an anonymous panegyric addressed to the emperor Constantine the Great (cf. p. 103 below) he is referred to as the prince of the Aedui, haranguing the senate, leaning on his long shield—a typical Gaulish orator. His mission was without success, however. He returned to Gaul, and in 58 B.C. he supported Caesar in his warfare against Ariovistus and the Bellovaci.[2] In his loyalty to the Roman cause he never wavered, while his brother Dumnorix was inexorably opposed to Caesar and a determined Gaulish nationalist. The policy and careers of these two brothers, as we follow them in Caesar's *Gallic War*, give us an intimate insight into

1 Münzer's account (Pauly–Wissowa, *R.-E.*, vol. v, 1, 1903, col. 1239, s.v. *Divitiacus*) of the passage in Cicero is misleading. We have no evidence that Divitiacus gave Cicero information about Gaulish customs and institutions, religion and culture, though this is not impossible.

2 The most powerful among the more civilized of the Belgic tribes. See W. Warde Fowler, *Julius Caesar* (London and New York, 1892), p. 168.

the personal problems which beset Gaulish family, no less than public, life in the Age of Invasions, both Roman and barbarian. I have added a brief outline of the careers of Divitiacus and Dumnorix as an appendix at the close of the present study.

Apart from Divitiacus (cf. pp. 103 ff. below) the political life of the druids in Gaul is little known. Dio Chrysostom, a contemporary of Tacitus, Lucan, and Suetonius, gives us a lofty picture of their power, in a passage claiming that the most powerful nations have appointed philosophers to act as controllers and officers for their kings, such as the *magi* for the Persians, the priests for the Egyptians, the Brahmins for the Indians, and he adds:

> The Celts appointed druids, who likewise were versed in the art of seers (περὶ μαντικὴν ὄντας) and other forms of wisdom (καὶ τὴν ἄλλην σοφίαν) without whom the kings were not permitted to adopt or plan any course, so that in fact it was these who ruled and the kings became their subordinates and instruments of their judgment, while themselves seated on golden thrones, and dwelling in great houses and being sumptuously feasted.[1]

Dio Chrysostom was a rhetorician, and the passage has a rhetorical flavour. The French scholar Dottin,[2] and also Kendrick,[3] were inclined to place little value on the statement, claiming that nothing confirms it for ancient times. Kendrick argues that Dio was an orator, not an historian, and had not travelled in Gaul. Nevertheless Dio's statement suggests that the account of the druids by Strabo and Caesar as judges and powerful political forces was still a living tradition among the Greek sophists in the late first and early second century A.D. Incidentally it is interesting to note the distinction made by Dio between priests and druids.

The reference to the rhetoric of Dio Chrysostom, following on the allusion to Divitiacus in the anonymous Latin panegyric addressed to Constantine (cf. p. 103 below), raises an interesting question. To what extent has the diction of

[1] *Oratio* xlix. [2] Op. cit., p. 382. [3] Op. cit., pp. 93 f.

Gaulish panegyrics affected the pictures of the druids, especially in the accounts of those concerned in their suppression? In the inflated passage in which Tacitus describes the superstitious practices on Anglesey he uses the poetical adjective *saevus*. Is he echoing a lost panegyric on Suetonius Paulinus and his conquest of the island and destruction of its 'groves'? There must have been many panegyrics—Latin, possibly also Gaulish—composed on Caesar during his conquest of Gaul, and we may be sure that the current descriptions of the human sacrifices of the Gauls would lose nothing in such tributes to the conqueror. Pliny may be indebted to one of these in the passage cited below (p. 70). The rhetorical style is especially characteristic of Lucan, and has infused the exalted passage in which he speaks of the teaching of the druids on the immortality of the soul to which reference will be made below.

IV

The Intellectual Activities of the Druids · The Alexandrian Tradition

FAR more interesting than the duties of the druids as augurs and diviners are their intellectual activities. As we have seen (p. 18 above), they were regarded from the earliest times as the philosophers of the Gauls, and this quality is especially stressed in later times by the Alexandrians, though it did not begin with them and was certainly not confined to them.

To define more narrowly the philosophical speculations of the druids, we may refer again to the brief references to this aspect contained in the works of the first century B.C. We have seen that according to Diodorus Siculus they were called the philosophers and theologians of the Gauls.[1] He asserts, perhaps following Polyhistor[2] (cf. p. 61 below), that 'the Pythagorean doctrine prevails among the Gauls' teaching that the souls of men are immortal (*ψυχὰς ἀθανάτους*), and after a fixed number of years they will enter into another body (*εἰς ἕτερον σῶμα τῆς ψυχῆς εἰσδυομένης*).[3] Although the druids are not specifically mentioned in this passage, there can be no doubt, in view of the statements of Strabo, Caesar, Mela, and Ammianus, about to be considered, that the statement of Diodorus refers to their teaching.

Strabo is more specific, though to be read in close connexion with Diodorus. 'The druids and others', he tells us, 'joined to the study of nature (cf. pp. 18 f. above) that of moral philosophy (*ἡ ἠθικὴ φιλοσοφία*), asserting that the human soul is indestructible, and also the universe, but that some

[1] v. 31. 2.

[2] See Ihm, in Pauly–Wissowa, *R.-E.* (s.v. *Druidae*), loc. cit., col. 1732.

[3] v. 28. 6.

time or other, fire and water will prevail' (cf. p. 20 above).[1] According to Caesar the druids taught the youths who came to them for instruction (cf. p. 44 above) 'many things respecting the stars and their motion, respecting the greatness (or size, *magnitudo*) of the world and of the earth, respecting the nature of things (*natura rerum*), respecting the power and majesty of the immortal gods'.[2]

Indeed the most interesting aspect of the druidical teaching, and the one which made most impression on the ancients from the earliest to the latest times is their view of the nature and destiny of the soul. According to Caesar: 'They desire to inculcate as their leading tenet, that souls do not become extinct, but pass after death from these present to those beyond,[3] and they hold that men by this are in a great degree incited to valour, the fear of death being disregarded.'[4] So also Pomponius Mela; and again the whole passage seems like an echo of Caesar or his source: 'One of the things which they teach has become common knowledge, namely that men's souls are everlasting, and enter upon another life among the shades of the departed; and this they declare so that men should be the better for the wars.'[5] We may add further, Ammianus Marcellinus (after Timagenes): 'The druids, men of loftier intellect [i.e. than the *vates*], and united to the intimate fraternity of the followers of Pythagoras, were absorbed by investigations into matters secret and sublime, and, unmindful of human affairs, declared souls to be immortal (*animas inmortales*).'[6] Strabo seeks to combine the druidical teaching on the immortality of the soul with the traditional, scientific learning, when he tells us that they claim that though souls are imperishable, and the world also, yet one day fire and water will prevail.[7]

[1] iv. 4. 4. [2] *Gallic War*, vi. 14.

[3] In primis hoc volunt persuadere, non interire animas, sed ab aliis post mortem transire ad alios. [4] *Gallic War*, vi. 14. [5] iii. 2. 19. [6] xv. 9. 8.

[7] iv. 4. 4. This is believed by Tierney (p. 223) to be derived from Posidonius, and is thought to be due to a tendency on his part to find analogies to Greek thought among the Gaulish druids. In this Posidonius was surely right.

The doctrines of the Celts were, in their essential features, well known, as Pomponius Mela says. The doctrine of the invalidity of death, the immortality of the soul and its rebirth, and the important part played by the druids as the repositories of the knowledge of the gods, are known to Lucan, who also stresses what must have been one of the chief attractions of the teaching of the druids—the complete absence of Hades, or of any ultimate system of punishment.[1]

You also, ye poets, who in your panegyrics hand down through the ages brave souls cut off in battle, free from apprehension have ye bards poured forth your wealth of song.[2] And you, ye druids, having laid aside your arms,[3] have returned to your barbaric rites and sinister mode of worship.—To you alone it is granted or withheld to have knowledge of the gods and the powers of heaven,[4] you who dwell in deep woods in sequestered groves. Your teaching is that the shades of the dead do not make their way to the silent abode of Erebus or the lightless realm of Dis below, but that the same soul animates the limbs in another sphere.[5] If you sing of certainties, death is the centre of continuous life. Truly the peoples on whom the Pole star looks down are happy in their error, for they are not harassed by the greatest of terrors, the fear of death. This gives the warrior his eagerness to rush upon the

[1] *Pharsalia*, i. 441 ff.

[2] Getty (*M. Annaei Lucani, De Bello Civili, Liber I* ad loc. (Cambridge, 1940)) compares the wording of Ammianus Marcellinus xv. 9. 8: 'Et Bardi quidem', &c. Cf. p. 52 above.

[3] 'Vous avez repris loin des armes vos rites', &c. Bourgery (*Lucain*, ed. Budé, vol. i, Paris, 1926) translates 'dans un autre monde'; but see Getty, op. cit., ad loc.

[4] 'i.e. your opinions about the gods differ so much from those of other nations, that either you have knowledge and no others have it, or vice versa' (Haskins, *Lucani Pharsalia* (London, 1887), note ad loc.). 'Their belief is so unlike that of other peoples that, if they are right, all others are wrong' (J. D. Duff, *Lucan* (London, 1928), note ad loc.); but I think that the passage refers rather to the divination of the druids. Bourgery translates: 'A vous seuls est donné de connaître les dieux et les puissances du ciel, ou à vous seuls de les ignorer.' See, however, note by Getty, ad loc.

[5] 'In a new cycle', Haskins (ed. cit., p. 26), who compares Virgil, *Aeneid*, vi. 748, and Conington's note to the passage. But is the use of *orbs* here certainly temporal? Duff (*Lucan*, ed. cit.), translates 'in a different scene'. Lejay and others translate 'in some other region'. We may compare the use of *orbs* in St. Paula's letter (Hieron. *Ep.* xlvi. 1, ed. Migne, *P.L.* vol. xxii, col. 490). See also Getty's note ad loc.

steel, a spirit ready to face death, and an indifference to save a life which will return.

Lucan's source, as we have already observed, is very probably related to the same source as Caesar's, which is echoed again later by Pomponius Mela. It should be emphasized, however, that the statement that the belief in immortality was a stimulus to the Gaulish warriors is merely a surmise of Caesar, Mela, and Lucan and their source, and is not to be interpreted as necessarily, or even probably, a motive of the druids. We may refer here to a passage in Athenaeus,[1] on the authority of Posidonius, according to which the Gauls, in exchange for money and wine, and certain guarantees that these should be divided among their relatives and friends, voluntarily submitted to decapitation by the sword. The Scholiast[2] refers to the Gaulish custom of selling their lives for money, and, after a year of feasting, allowing themselves to be stoned to death by the populace. Again, however, there is no specific reference to the druids, but such a custom must have rested on a belief in immortality of some kind which the druids evidently held and taught. Valerius Maximus, writing at about the beginning of the first century A.D., mentions it as currently stated to be an old custom among the Gauls, that 'they lent sums of money to each other which are repayable in the next world, so firmly are they convinced that the souls of men are immortal'; and he identifies their views in this respect with those ascribed by the Greeks to Pythagoras.[3] Here again the druids are not specifically mentioned, but there can be no doubt that the passage, like those referred to above, rests on the belief in immortality such as was inculcated by the druids.

1 iv. 154 c.

2 Lactantius Placidus, *Commentarius in Statii Thebaida*, ed. R. Jahnke (Leipzig, 1898), x, no. 793.

3 Vetus ille mos Gallorum occurrit, quos memoria proditum est pecunias mutuas, quae his apud inferos redderentur, dare, quia persuasum habuerint animas hominum immortales esse. Dicerem stultos, nisi idem bracati sensissent, quod palliatus Pythagoras credidit (*Factorum et Dictorum Memorabilium Libri Novem*, ii. 6. 10).

It has been necessary to stress these details of the tenets of the druids at this point because they have an important bearing on, and indeed perhaps give us the clue to, the place of the druids as partakers in the peripheral philosophical thought of the ancient world. The views which they express are doubtless in some cases uniform with the views of Posidonius. In a number of other cases however they name their own source, which is quite different. We have seen that Diodorus states categorically that among the Gauls the opinion prevails that souls are immortal, and after a number of years enter upon a new life, passing into another body; and this opinion he attributes to the teaching of Pythagoras. There is in fact no certainty that the words of either Diodorus or Caesar refer specifically to the transmigration of souls in the commonly accepted sense of the term, which incidentally finds no echo in Strabo, and is interpreted very differently by Mela and evidently also by Lucan. Among these writers the tradition of the immortality of the soul may refer rather to its subsequent life in another state or in another sphere, as suggested by some of the earlier Ionian philosophers. But it is evident that already by the first century B.C. the belief in the immortality of the soul was interpreted to indicate a belief in transmigration, and to have been derived from so-called Pythagorean doctrines. We have just seen that Valerius Maximus, who wrote about the beginning of the century, notes what he regards as the identity of the views of the Gauls on the survival of the soul with those of Pythagoras.[1]

On the other hand Ammianus Marcellinus,[2] who also suggests that the druids subscribed to the doctrine of the Pythagoreans, and appears to speak of corporate associations of druids analogous to the Pythagorean associations, gives as his authority Timagenes, who probably wrote about the middle of the first century B.C., and who is reported by

[1] Loc. cit.

[2] *Hist. Rom.* xv. 9. 8. The passage is not easy to translate. For the syntax and interpretation see G. Dottin, *L'Antiquité celtique*, pp. 377 f.

Ammianus himself (cf. p. 86 below) to have been a research worker in older written sources.

In this section of his discussion Professor Tierney's views are perhaps open to question, for while claiming that our knowledge of the druids as philosophers is based on Posidonius he also claims (p. 223) that Posidonius' account of the druids cannot possibly in this respect be authentic, partly on the ground that some of their practices are incompatible with the rarefied levels of Greek philosophy ascribed to them by Posidonius himself. He maintains that the alleged studies of the druids are simply a programme of Stoic philosophy, including some of their specific doctrines, such as that of the periodic destruction of the universe by fire and water. 'The picture of the Druids then is not historical' (loc. cit.). And Tierney adds: 'It is difficult to believe that the druids possessed any body of coherent religious doctrine much less the philosophy, so liberally bestowed on them by Posidonius.' As a further argument Tierney refers to a recent study by Vendryes of 'Gallic religion', which 'is rather one of multiplicity and diversity than of anything remotely resembling a system'. Finally, Tierney regards 'the Pythagorean belief in the immortality of the soul, with its peculiar utilitarian motivation of valour in battle' as having been 'superimposed' on the druids to illustrate the reckless valour of the Celts.

If we were indeed solely dependent on the work of Posidonius for our knowledge of the doctrines of the druids it might be difficult to disagree with Professor Tierney on the doctrinaire tone of our earliest writers on this matter. It is perhaps hardly necessary to refute his argument that the combination of certain savage national customs is incompatible with lofty ideas. The reverse can be illustrated among many peoples, including the Greeks and Romans themselves. That the studies attributed to the druids are also recognizable elements in Stoic philosophy one would not for a moment deny; and on the other hand neither would one seriously maintain that the teaching of the druids possessed any body of coherent philosophy, and far less of religious doctrine. Of the latter, in fact, we hear very little. Finally the doctrine of immortality attributed to them is hardly likely to have had exclusive reference to Celtic valour in battle, which is at best a conjecture of later foreign (i.e. non-Celtic) writers.

As against the common and, as it seems to me, facile definition of the druids as priests (*clergé*) and druidism as a religious organization,[1] and in opposition to the philosophy denied to them by Professor Tierney, I would endorse the view expressed by Ferdinand Lot in his brief survey of 'Le Druidisme':

> Les druides ne sont pas une caste . . . ils ne sont pas même, à proprement parler, un clergé, bien qu'ils président aux sacrifices, dont les sacrifices humains. Confrérie de 'sages' à la manière antique, c'est-à-dire d'intermédiaires entre l'homme et la Divinité, ils exercent la divination, la magie, ces pratiques étant réservées à une subdivision de *l'ordo*, les *euhages* ou *ouateïs*. Mais aussi et surtout, ils détiennent une conception du monde et de la destinée posthume de l'humanité qui fait d'eux des philosophes, philosophes barbares, tout de même des philosophes.[2]

The fact is that one would not look for a coherent system of thought among the Gauls or any other Celtic peoples of the period to which the druids belong. What one might at best expect would be a share in the current views of the intelligentsia of the Western Mediterranean world, orally and therefore imperfectly transmitted, orally learnt and imperfectly apprehended, but nevertheless partaking in essence of the great systems of the past and present. Their ideas could be no more than the outer ripple on the circumference from the great centres of thought elsewhere. Even these faint outer ripples would tend to be contaminated by old traditional ideas, and old customs of a past (ancient) phase of thought long established in the country, while now receiving a new superimposed layer. We can not hope to build up a 'system'

[1] As claimed by J. Vendryes, *La Religion des Celtes* (Paris, 1948), pp. 291 f.

[2] F. Lot, *La Gaule* (Paris, 1947), p. 76. Cf. also the view of Dottin (p. 45 above).

which could not, and never did, exist among the druids, and still less must we confuse their philosophical conceptions with the 'religion' of the Gauls. The two are totally different, so far as we can judge by the evidence of our sources.

In addition to our knowledge of the druids from works of the first century B.C., which are admittedly largely derived from Posidonius, we also possess another body of tradition, less comprehensive, less—so it appears—direct, and again not, so far as we know, preserved in any works composed by travellers who had been in Gaul. Partly for these reasons, and partly because of their secondary nature, this second series of traditions is apt to be either overlooked, or treated as late in origin and therefore as relatively unimportant. The traditions of this group are commonly preserved in Greek texts written by scholars educated in the School of Alexandria from at least as early as the first century A.D. onwards. Fortunately these relatively late authors not infrequently mention the names of the authorities from whose written texts they claim to be deriving their material.

This does not, of course, involve us in believing that a given writer in question is necessarily quoting his alleged source at first hand. Such a meticulous citing of authorities is a modern standard of scholarship to which these writers would have made no claim. They were members of a school largely devoted to the compilation of encyclopedias, and the ideals of such are the dissemination of ascertained knowledge rather than the part played by the individual in its source. Nevertheless from the nature of the sources actually cited, whether directly or only at second hand, we are enabled to ascertain that much of this Alexandrian material is, at least in origin, as early as the tradition derived from Posidonius, some of it apparently earlier, as we shall see.

This Alexandrian tradition and its dating can be checked at times when the writers, quite independently of one another, and even separated by long intervals of time, can be shown to have made use of a common early source. The importance of the Alexandrian tradition is therefore great. Its special value lies not least in the fact that it is fundamentally different in tone and emphasis from the Posidonian tradition, for it refers to the druids with respect, and discusses their philosophy on the level of other systems beyond the limits of the Ionian and the Greek world. Whereas the Posidonian tradition incorporates elements unfavourable to the druids, the Alexandrian, however erroneous at times in the interpretation of the traditions, is in tone respectful towards the druids. There is little contradiction of fact between the two classes of evidence, but the emphasis and climate are totally different. The 'Alexandrians' are not concerned with discreditable practices, such as human sacrifice, but with the lofty ideals and investigations of the druids, which they, no less than Posidonius, connect with the Pythagoreans.

Already *c.* A.D. 100 Dio Chrysostom who, as we have seen, speaks with the highest respect of the political influence of the druids, is no less respectful towards their intellectual attainments, crediting them with concerning themselves with the mantic art and the other branches of wisdom (*καὶ τούτους περὶ μαντικὴν ὄντας καὶ τὴν ἄλλην σοφίαν*), and speaking of them as on a level with the *magi* of the Persians, the priests of the Egyptians, and the Brahmins of the Indians.[1]

From the time of Dio Chrysostom onwards it becomes a habit among the 'Alexandrians' to speak of the druids of the Gauls in close context with the early philosophers of the great civilizations of the ancients, notably the Persians, the Egyptians, and the Brahmins of India, and finally the Pythagoreans. Hippolytus, for example, writing in the late second or early third century A.D., claimed that the druids had adopted the teaching of Pythagoras through the intermediacy of his slave Zalmoxis of Thrace, who, according to Herodotus[2] had been a slave of Pythagoras in Samos, and who ultimately

[1] *Oratio* xlix. 7, 8 (ed. H. L. Crosby, London and Harvard, 1846).
[2] iv. 94 f. Cf. Strabo, vii. 3. 5.

returned to Thrace[1] with wealth and prestige, and promised the Getae immortality for himself and the chief men of their clan and their descendants, and was ultimately worshipped by the Getae as their god.

> The druids among the Celts having profoundly examined the Pythagorean philosophy, Zalmoxis, a Thracian by race, the slave of Pythagoras, having become for them the founder of this discipline, he after the death of Pythagoras, having made his way there [? sc. to Thrace[2]], became the founder of this philosophy for them. The Celts honour them as prophets and prognosticators because they foretell matters by the ciphers and numbers according to the Pythagorean skill. . . . The druids also practise magic arts however.[3]

In view of the tradition recorded by Herodotus it was in no way unnatural that Hippolytus should associate the belief of the druids in immortality with the Pythagorean doctrine. The sources of Hippolytus[4] are not believed to have been confined to one author. Among others Diogenes Laertius is frequently quoted in support of his statements. No authority is cited for the statements about the druids, but Diogenes Laertius and Clement of Alexandria contain statements which bear some similarity to those made by Hippolytus shortly before our passage, and may probably be derived from the same source. In fact, however, Clement of Alexandria reverses the debt as stated by Hippolytus, claiming that philosophy had its beginnings among the barbarians (cf. p. 61 below).

Clement of Alexandria, speaking of philosophy as having

[1] The exact meaning of ἐκεῖ is not quite clear. Does it refer to Thrace, and is this regarded by Hippolytus as part of the country of the Celts?

[2] On this interpretation of the text see E. R. Dodds, *The Greeks and the Irrational* (University of California, reprint 1963), p. 165, n. 60.

[3] *Δρυΐδαι οἱ ἐν Κελτοῖς τῇ Πυθαγορείῳ φιλοσοφίᾳ κατ' ἄκρον ἐγκύψαντες, αἰτίου αὐτοῖς γενομένου ταύτης τῆς ἀσκήσεως Ζαλμόξιδος δούλου Πυθαγόρου γένει Θρᾳκίου, ὃς μετὰ τὴν Πυθαγόρου τελευτὴν ἐκεῖ χωρήσας αἴτιος τούτοις ταύτης τῆς φιλοσοφίας ἐγένετο. τούτοις Κελτοὶ ὡς προφήτας καὶ προγνωστικοὺς δοξάζουσιν, διὰ τὸ ἐκ ψήφων καὶ ἀριθμῶν Πυθαγορικῇ τέχνῃ προαγορεύειν αὐτοῖς τινα. . . . χρῶνται δὲ δρυΐδαι καὶ μαγείαις* (Hippolytus, *Philosophumena*, i. 22).

[4] See the note by F. Legge in his translation of *Philosophumena*, vol. i (London, 1921), p. 64, n. 2.

flourished of old among the barbarians, specifies the 'druids of the Gauls' (*Γαλατῶν οἱ δρυΐδαι*) as outstanding examples. Incidentally in the same list he also specifies the 'philosophers of the Celts' (*Κελτῶν οἱ φιλοσοφήσαντες*), and it may be observed in passing that the *Galatae* and *Keltae* were terms used synonymously by Strabo[1] and Diodorus[2] and also by later writers (cf. p. 63 below), and doubtless the identification goes back to an early common source. But Clement expresses the extravagant claim—on what authority we are not specifically told—that Pythagoras and the Greeks have acquired philosophy from the Gauls and other barbarians.[3]

This extravagant claim excepted, Clement seems to be indebted to Polyhistor in his passage relating to the connexion between the Gauls and Pythagoras, for he cites a book by Alexander (i.e. Alexander Cornelius Polyhistor) on the *Symbols of Pythagoras* shortly before this passage.[4] Polyhistor was roughly contemporary with Timagenes, and like him a writer deriving his materials from earlier sources. These two writers, then, Timagenes and Polyhistor, both writing about the middle of the first century B.C., are using material which is in all probability older, and certainly not later than the record of Posidonius.

Clement's testimony is particularly important for several reasons. After claiming that philosophy had formerly flourished among the barbarians, and had been transmitted by them to the Greeks, he passes on to enumerate the ancient civilizations among whom it had flourished, specifying the prophets of the Egyptians, the 'Chaldeans' of the Assyrians, the druids of the Gauls, the 'shamans' of the Bactrians, those who practised philosophy among the Celts (*Κελτῶν οἱ φιλοσοφήσαντες*), and

[1] '*Galatia* or *Gaul*'. Cf., e.g., 'the whole race which is now called both "*Gallic*" and "*Galatae*"', iv. 4. 2; cf. further ii. 5. 28; iv. 1. 1, 5, 14; 3. 2.

[2] Cf., e.g., v. 24; xvii. 113; xxv. 13.

[3] *Stromata*, i. 15. 71 (ed. L. Früchtel, Berlin, 1960), p. 45.

[4] Ibid., i. 15. 70 (ed. Früchtel, p. 44). For the passage cited from Alexander Cornelius Polyhistor, see F. Jacoby, *F. Gr. Hist.* IIIA (Leiden, 1940), no. 94 (p. 118). For the estimate in which Polyhistor was held by the ancients see Jacoby, *F. Gr. Hist.* III a (Leiden, 1943), no. 273, pp. 248 ff.

the *magi* of the Persians.[1] Shortly before this passage, he speaks of Pythagoras as having been a disciple of [Na]zaratus the Assyrian. And for this information he cites as his source Alexander (sc. Polyhistor) in his book *De Symbolis Pythagoricis*.[2] Evidently at least one of Clement's sources for information about the druids and their Pythagorean doctrines is Polyhistor.

But we are not left to conjecture as to Clement's direct source of information about the druids. The fifth-century Christian archbishop of Alexandria, St. Cyril, in his thesis *Contra Julianum*, quotes what would seem to be the identical passage cited above by Clement, and categorically states Polyhistor's book *The Symbols of Pythagoras* as his source. Here also we find the same distinction made between the Gauls and the Celts, and here the barbarian races are honoured for their share in probity, justice, and philosophy.[3] The lists of Clement and Cyril are worth closer comparison:

Clement of Alexandria[4]	*Cyril of Alexandria*[5]	*Diogenes Laertius*[6]
Egyptians: Prophetae	Egyptians { Philosophati, Prophetae	Persians: Magi
Assyrians: Chaldaei	Assyrians: Chaldaei	Babylonians, Assyrians } Chaldaei
Galatai (Gauls): Druidae	Gauls: Druidaei	Indians: Gymnosophistae
Bactrians: Samanaei[7]	Bactrians, Persians } Samanaei	
Celts: Philosophati		
Persians: Magi	Celts: non pauci [sc.: Philosophati]	Celts and Galatae } Druidaei
Indians: Gymnosophistae	Persians: Magi	
	Indians: Gymnosophistae, &c.	

[1] *Stromata*, ed. cit., p. 45.

[2] Ibid., p. 44: *Ἀλέξανδρος δὲ ἐν τῷ περὶ Πυθαγορικῶν συμβόλων Ζαράτῳ τῷ Ἀσσυρίῳ μαθητεῦσαι ἱστορεῖ τὸν Πυθαγόραν . . . ἀκηκοέναι τε πρὸς τούτοις Γαλατῶν καὶ βραχμάνων τὸν Πυθαγόραν βούλεται.*

[3] *βαρβάρους γε μήν, οὐχὶ δὲ μάντεις ἁπλῶς ἀγρίους ἥκοντας δὲ πρὸς τοῦτο χρηστότητος καὶ ἐπιεικείας ἔσθ' ὅτε τινάς, ὥστε καὶ ἀξιοζήλωτον ὄνομα λαχεῖν. Ἱστορεῖ γοῦν Ἀλέξανδρος ὁ ἐπίκλην Πολυΐστωρ ἐν τῷ Περὶ Πυθαγορικῶν συμβόλων, Ἀσσυρίῳ τὸ γένος ὄντι τῷ Ζάρᾳ φοιτῆσαι τὸν Πυθαγόραν, κτλ*, *Contra Julianum*, iv (ed. Migne, *P.G.*, vol. lxxvi, col. 705).

[4] For the sake of convenience the list is given in the Latin form from the edition in Migne, *P.G.*, vol. viii, col. 778. For the Greek cf. Früchtel, ed. cit., p. 45.

[5] St. Cyril of Alexandria, *Contra Julianum*, loc. cit.

[6] Book i, Preface.

[7] i.e. Shamans.

Clement closes his list with some brief additional notes on Anacharsis of Thrace and the vegetarian habits of the Hyperboreans. This passage also has verbal correspondence with that of Cyril, who also concludes his list[1] with the names of Anacharsis among the *philosophati* of the Scythians, and of Zalmoxis in Thrace, and adds that some of the Hyperboreans who dwell beyond the Rhipean mountains practise justice and live as vegetarians.[2] Cyril's passage is obviously derived from the same source as Clement's. It seems clear, however, from a close comparison of both content and expression that Cyril has not derived his passage directly from Clement.

It will be noticed that not only are the two lists of Clement and Cyril given above virtually identical in content, but that they also follow the same order. Clearly, therefore, Clement and Cyril derived their information about the Pythagorean tenets of the Gaulish druids and their exaltation, along with the thesis that philosophy began with the barbarians, from Polyhistor or one of his sources. Cyril, however, says nothing of the Greeks and Pythagoras specifically having derived their philosophy from the Gauls and other barbarians; and Diogenes, as we shall see, directly contradicts it. Clement perhaps derived this statement from some source other than Polyhistor. He may, indeed, be merely conjecturing. The list cited by Diogenes Laertius, while much briefer, and following a slightly different order, nevertheless corresponds closely so far as it goes with those of Clement and Cyril, and has no contradictory elements. Probably a common original source lies behind all three, and has been the source of Polyhistor himself. Origen also cites Celsus as numbering the Hyperboreans side by side with Odrysians, Samothracians, and Eleusinians as 'among the most ancient and wise nations', and the 'Galactophagi' of Homer, the druids of

[1] Loc. cit.

[2] *φασὶ δέ τινας καὶ τῶν Ὑπερβοραίων ἐθνῶν τοὺς ὑπὲρ τὰ Ῥιπαῖα κατῳκηκότας ὄρη δικαιοσύνης γενέσθαι μελεδωνοὺς καὶ ὀψοφαγίας ἀποφοιτᾷν, καὶ διαίτης μὲν οὐκ ἀνέχεσθαι Συβαριτικῆς, ἀγαπᾷν δὲ μόνην τῶν ἀκροδρύων τὴν χρῆσιν.*

the Gauls, and the Getae as 'very wise and ancient nations'.[1] We know that Origen owed much to Clement of Alexandria whose works he had read and whose point of view he had absorbed.[2]

Now Diogenes Laertius was evidently aware of the tradition reported and endorsed by Clement that philosophy was borrowed by the Greeks from the barbarians, for he refers to it in the opening words of his prologue: 'There are some who say that the study of philosophy had its beginning among the barbarians.'[3]

He then immediately adds that they cite in support of their belief the list which I have quoted above, and that they refer as their authorities to the *Magicus* of Aristotle, and to Sotion in his book of the *Succession of Philosophers*. Diogenes, however, claims that the achievements which they attribute to the barbarians belong in reality to the Greeks; and again later in the prologue he adds: 'It was from the Greeks that philosophy took its rise: its very name refuses to be translated into foreign speech.'[4]

Diogenes, it will be observed, does not cite Polyhistor as the immediate source of his list. Nevertheless, he cites a passage (cf. pp. 60, 61 above) which corresponds on general lines with the one from Polyhistor referred to above, and used by both Clement and Cyril. In this passage Diogenes states that 'the Persians had their *magi*, the Babylonians or the Assyrians their *Chaldaeans*, the Indians their *Gymnosophists*, while the Celts and the Galatae had men called *δρυΐδαι* and *Σεμνοθέοι*'.[5] On the authority of Diogenes also, the well-known sixth-century scholar Stephanus of Byzantium, mentions the druids as the philosophers of the Gauls (*δρυΐδαι ἔθνος Γαλατικὸν φιλόσοφον, ὡς Λαέρτιος Διογένης ἐν φιλοσόφῳ ἱστορίᾳ*).[6]

[1] *σοφώτατα λέγει ἔθνη εἶναι καὶ ἀρχαῖα* (*Contra Celsum*, i. 16).

[2] See H. Chadwick, *Contra Celsum* (Cambridge, 1953), p. ix.

[3] *τὸ τῆς φιλοσοφίας ἔργον ἔνιοί φασιν ἀπὸ βαρβάρων ἄρξαι.*

[4] *καὶ ὧδε μὲν ἀφ' Ἑλλήνων ἦρξε φιλοσοφία, ἧς καὶ αὐτὸ ὄνομα τὴν βάρβαρον ἀπέστραπται προσηγορίαν.*

[5] *Lives of the Philosophers*, i, Preface 1.

[6] *Ἐθνικῶν* (edited by A. Westermann, Leipzig, 1839), p. 107.

Diogenes cites as his authorities on the druids, however, two works, one by Sotion the Peripatetic (*fl. c.* 190 B.C.) from the 23rd book of his compilation entitled *Διαδοχὴ τῶν φιλοσόφων*; the other, now lost, by an anonymous writer of *c.* 200 B.C. citing an apocryphal treatise, with the title of *Μαγικός*,[1] falsely ascribed to Aristotle.

The tradition quoted by Diogenes, therefore, and given by Clement and Cyril from Polyhistor (*c.* 50 B.C.) is given by Diogenes on the authority of two works of *c.* 200 B.C. As Kendrick has pointed out[2] it apparently goes back therefore in written form to a period before the Roman occupation of Gaul, and is probably considerably earlier than the period *c.* 200 B.C. when it was evidently already in a written text. And Kendrick justly adds: 'To have had even this much of reputation outside their own Keltic world in the second century before Christ the druids must have been already long-established.'[3]

It would seem then that for the high estimate of the druids as ranking among the philosophers of the great races of antiquity which we have found current among the Alexandrians, we may in all probability go back to written sources of at least as early as the third century B.C. which Polyhistor is also presumably citing in his own work.

This does not, however, include all the source material used by Polyhistor on the druids. Clement also quotes him as his authority for the close relationship between the druids and Pythagoras: 'Alexander (Polyhistor) desires to state that . . . Pythagoras was one of those who hearkened to the Galatae and the Brahmins.'[4] And Cyril, though less specific, seems

[1] See V. Rose, *Aristoteles Pseudepigraphus* (Leipzig, 1863), pp. 51, 52. Id., *Aristotelis . . . Fragmenta* (Leipzig, 1886), pp. 43 f.: *τὸ τῆς φιλοσοφίας ἔργον ἔνιοί φασιν ἀπὸ βαρβάρων ἄρξαι. γεγενῆσθαι γὰρ παρὰ μὲν Πέρσαις Μάγους, παρὰ δὲ Βαβυλωνίοις ἢ Ἀσσυρίοις Χαλδαίους, καὶ Γυμνοσοφιστὰς παρ' Ἰνδοῖς, παρά τε Κελτοῖς καὶ Γαλάταις τοὺς καλουμένους Δρυΐδας καὶ Σεμνοθέους, καθά φησιν Ἀριστοτέλης ἐν τῷ Μαγικῷ καὶ Σωτίων ἐν Εἰκοστῷ τρίτῳ τῆς Διαδοχῆς*. Diogenes Laertius Book I, Preface. Cf. also Zwicker, *Fontes Historiae Religionis Celticae*, i (Berlin, 1934), p. 8.

[2] Op. cit., p. 75.

[3] Loc. cit.

[4] *Stromata*, i. 15. 70. 1.

vaguely to suggest a connexion. Hippolytus states more fully that the druids of the Kelts were followers of Pythagoras (via Zalmoxis), but cites no authority. It would seem, therefore, that for his information on the connexion of the druids with Pythagorean philosophy Polyhistor must have obtained some of his information from some other source than the Pseudo-Aristotle or the book by Sotion. Where did he obtain it?

The *locus classicus* for our early information about Pythagoras and the Pythagoreans is a well-known passage in Diogenes Laertius (viii. 26–50). At the beginning of chapter 25 Diogenes states his source thus: 'Alexander [sc. Polyhistor] in his *Successions of Philosophers* says that he found in the Pythagorean memoirs the following tenets as well.'[1]

It is clear that Diogenes has taken Polyhistor as his chief authority on the doctrines of Pythagoras,[2] and in fact Polyhistor is known to have written a special work on the Pythagorean system, to which Diogenes probably had access, and which he evidently regarded as the most trustworthy authority, to the exclusion of the large output of Neopythagorean literature published between the work of Polyhistor in the first century B.C., and the third century A.D., in which he himself was writing.[3]

Again in chapter 36 Diogenes refers to the same source: 'This is what Alexander says that he found in the Pythagorean memoirs. What follows is Aristotle's.'[4]

The editor points out[5] that the use of the word *εὑρηκέναι* in both passages indicates that in the Lives of Pythagoras which Diogenes is using the second extract from Alexander Polyhistor has displaced a passage which came from the spurious Aristotelian treatise *Περὶ Πυθαγορείων*.

[1] *φησι δ' Ἀλέξανδρος ἐν ταῖς τῶν φιλοσόφων διαδοχαῖς καὶ ταῦτα εὑρηκέναι ἐν Πυθαγορικοῖς ὑπομνήμασιν*. Cf. also cap. 36.

[2] See R. D. Hicks, *Diogenes Laertius*, vol. ii (London and Cambridge, Mass., 1958), p. 340, note *a*.

[3] Hicks, loc. cit.

[4] *καὶ ταῦτα μέν φησιν ὁ Ἀλέξανδρος ἐν τοῖς Πυθαγορικοῖς ὑπομνήμασιν εὑρηκέναι, καὶ τὰ ἐκείνων ἐχόμενα ὁ Ἀριστοτέλης.*

[5] Cf. Hicks, ed. cit., p. 350, note *c*.

As to the date and authenticity of the Pythagorean memoirs (*Πυθαγορικὰ ὑπομνήματα*) cited by Diogenes from Alexander Polyhistor, opinion has varied greatly, but the account of Diogenes based on this authority is relatively sober as compared with later accounts of Neopythagoreans. As Guthrie points out[1] the *Πυθαγορικὰ ὑπομνήματα* which he cites as his source recall the *ὑπομνήματα κεφαλαιώδη* handed down by the Pythagoreans in the fourth century B.C., at a period when, after the middle of the fifth century, the Pythagorean School had ceased to exist as a united body, but continued in the form of scattered communities over a wide area of the Hellenistic world, and as a natural consequence developed certain variations of doctrine.[2]

On the date or dates of the contents of these Pythagorean notebooks scholars are far from agreement. Strong arguments have been put forward for a date in the fourth century B.C., while a third and even a second century date have found favour.[3] On the whole the earlier date is regarded by the majority as probable, partly, but not wholly, on the ground of the relative sobriety of the documents. Raven has pointed out[4] that the account of Pythagoreanism preserved by Alexander Polyhistor (and known to us from Diogenes Laertius viii. 25; Diels–Kranz, *Fragmente der Vorsokratiker*, 58 B I a) from some otherwise unknown *Πυθαγορικὰ ὑπομνήματα* is remarkably compressed, but that if it were expanded in the manner that one of the commentators expanded the words of Aristotle it would seem to yield a complete and coherent picture of the evolution of the Pythagorean system during the fifth century. It is difficult to see how, if Polyhistor had based his account on the Pythagorean system of a later date, when differentiation had set in, his notes could be made consistent with the evidence of Aristotle. Whatever conclusion we reach,

1 *History of Greek Philosophy* (Cambridge, 1962), p. 201, n. 3.

2 Ibid., pp. 180 ff.

3 Full references to the scholars holding these views are given by Guthrie, loc. cit.

4 J. E. Raven, *Pythagoreans and Eleatics* (Cambridge, 1948), pp. 159 f., 163.

the latest possible date for sources used by Polyhistor is the second century B.C., and the account of Pythagoras given by Diogenes can be no later than that, even if Festugière were right in attributing the immediate source of Polyhistor's 'Pythagorean notes' to a Hellenistic compilation incorporating elements of diverse dates; but in the view of the two most recent writers, F. M. Cornford and Professor Guthrie, the extract by Diogenes from Polyhistor 'contains elements of genuine early Pythagorean doctrine'.[1] Raven himself, if I understand him aright, seems to favour the first half, and possibly the second quarter, of the fourth century B.C. for Polyhistor's *Πυθαγορικὰ ὑπομνήματα*,[2] and it has been argued cogently by Cornford and others[3] that even if the Pythagorean system as given by Polyhistor shows certain traces of anachronistic phraseology, these may well be due to Polyhistor himself rather than to his source.

[1] Guthrie, loc. cit. [2] Op. cit., p. 163. [3] See Guthrie, loc. cit.

V

The Decline of the Druids

WHEN we compare our material drawn from extant writers of the first century B.C. with material from the following century, it will be seen that there is a considerable change of tone, and this is the more remarkable since both Lucan and Mela are closely dependent on the former writers. That is to say they are writing in the Posidonian tradition. Yet even when they specifically recall the facts recorded in this tradition the emphasis has changed. The emphasis in our later writers is on secrecy and seclusion. The accent is no longer on the public activities of the druids as officials controlling public affairs, whether nation-wide meetings, or great public sacrifices, or as peacemakers between opposing armies, or even as 'just judges'. Instead we hear of their secret meetings and teaching in caves or forest groves. This aspect is particularly emphasized by Pliny, who gives us our only full-scale picture of a druid ceremony. It takes place in an oak grove, and he tells us that this is usual.

Side by side with the development of secrecy is the prominence given to magic and medicine, especially by Pliny. This has now become so integral a part of druidism that, as we have seen, for Professor Tierney (p. 215) 'the medico-magical side of the druids, so prominent in Pliny's *Natural History*, is the true historical basis of their power and influence'. Yet our earlier authorities on the druids lay no emphasis on the matter. Almost all that Pliny tells us of the druids might apply to a totally different class from the druids of earlier writers. While not inconsistent with what we know of the Gauls in general from other sources, it is entirely absent from the Posidonian tradition relating to the druids as far as this tradition is known to us from the sources already considered.

In addition to these changes noticeable in the functions of the druids there is also a change of tone in the writers of the first century A.D. The attitude of the records is less objective. The druids are no longer presented as a class of high status commanding respect even from their enemies. To Tacitus the sacrifices of Anglesey with which they are possibly associated are '*saevus*'; to Lucan their ceremonies are 'barbaric rites and a forbidding mode of worship'. To Mela 'there still remain some traces of their former savagery', and though Mela is here speaking of the Gauls, without specific mention of the druids, he refers to the druids in the next sentence; and he is virtually quoting Caesar. Suetonius refers to 'the barbarous and inhuman religion of the druids'. To him it was a *religio dirae immanitatis*. Pliny concludes his account of the druids with an unequivocal condemnation. 'We can hardly realize how much is owed to the Romans, who swept away the monstrous conditions, in which to kill a man was the highest religious function, and to eat him was even highly salubrious.'[1]

This change of tone is to be attributed to two causes. The first and most important is the decline of the prestige and acquirements of the druids themselves. Indeed it is safe to say that this had already begun well before Caesar wrote, and is a natural outcome of the political situation in Gaul resulting from the disintegration incidental to various foreign invasions and to Roman civilizing influences. The second—probably much less weighty—reason for the change of tone in references to the druids by writers of the first century A.D. lies in the attitude of the Roman senate and the policy of the Emperors in legislation for the newly conquered Gauls, and perhaps also the druids. In accordance with the general political and cultural aims of Rome to her subject peoples Augustus opened schools for Roman education in Gaul, the

[1] Pliny, xxx. 4.

most famous of which was founded *c.* 12 B.C. at Augustodunum which undoubtedly superseded the druidic school mentioned by Tacitus at the old Gaulish capital of the Aedui at Bibracte.[1] This measure served the primary and consistent Roman purpose of offering opportunities of Roman education and culture to the young Gauls, and we learn from the Latin panegyric poem[2] delivered by Eumenius of Autun before the governor of the province in 298 what a delightful university had been here provided for its young students. Inevitably it also served the purpose of attracting the clientele of young Gaulish nobles away from the teaching of the druids to a *milieu* which offered superior opportunities of advancement under the new régime. The measure must have reacted strongly in favour of the loyalty and submission of their parents to Rome, since their sons were now in a fair way to become technically Roman citizens. At the same time the effect of the opening up of Roman schools for the young Gaulish nobility must inevitably have been to strike at the heart of the influence of the druids.

It was undoubtedly as an element in this policy of integrating Gaul in the Empire that a series of repressive measures is reported to us as having been directed towards suppressing the power of the druids from the beginning of the Christian era onwards. First we learn from Suetonius[3] that Augustus passed a measure prohibiting druidical practices (*religio druidarum*) to 'Roman citizens', that is to say to those Gauls who had accepted citizenship in the Empire. Perhaps Suetonius himself has assigned the motive for the measure, which he states was the *religio dirae immanitatis* of the druids. But the Romans were accustomed to the gratuitous shedding

[1] Augustodunum caput gentis . . . nobilissimam Gallorum sobolem liberalibus studiis ibi operatam (Tacitus, *Annals*, iii. 43; cf. Suetonius, *De Grammaticis et Rhetoribus* 3). Augustodunum is the modern Autun.

[2] *Pro Instaurandis Scholis*, edited by Baehrens, *XII Panegyrici Latini* (Leipzig, 1911), pp. 248 ff.; *Panégyriques latins*, vol. i, text and French translation by E. Galletier (Paris, 1949), pp. 103 ff.

[3] *Lives of the Emperors*, v. The Deified Claudius, chap. xxv.

of blood in the arena, and Augustus had refrained on the whole from interfering with the beliefs of subject races.[1] We may well believe that he felt himself obliged to discountenance druidism because of its strong nationalist and anti-Roman force.[2] We may probably regard the druids as the most formidable nationalist and anti-Roman force with which the Romans had to contend.[3] In forbidding 'citizens' of the Empire to take part in druidical practices the object before Augustus was certainly to separate them from an influence which was strongly nationalistic.[4] Mommsen[5] stressed the important bearing of the fact that in the revolt of the Aedui and the Treveri, in the reign of Tiberius in A.D. 21, the insurgents sought above all to obtain Augustodunum, the capital of the Aedui, in order to obtain control of the youths studying there, and by this means to overawe the great families of Gaul.[6]

The measure discountenancing druidism by Augustus was a very mild one and cannot be regarded as a direct persecution of the order of the druids themselves. It was, however, only the first Roman political measure which we have on record as having been promulgated against them. In A.D. 16 *mathematici* and *magi* were expelled from Italy,[7] a measure which was doubtless primarily directed against the Pythagoreans, with whom, according to Alexandrian authorities, the druids had much in common. In A.D. 21 certain cities of the Gauls broke into revolt, chiefly on the ground of heavy financial exactions, and also, as is thought, possibly

1 Cf. M. Hadas, 'Nationalism under Hellenistic and Roman Imperialism', *Journal of the History of Ideas*, xi (1950), p. 138.

2 On this see A. D. Nock, *Cambridge Ancient History*, vol. x (Cambridge, 1934), p. 499.

3 For a recent expression of this view see V. M. Scramuzza, *The Emperor Claudius* (Harvard, 1940), pp. 206 ff., 308, n. 36. Scramuzza is not always judicial in his details, but his general assessment of the situation is sound.

4 Ibid., op. cit., p. 492.

5 *The Provinces of the Roman Empire* (translation by W. P. Dickson), vol. i, London, 1909, p. 112.

6 Tacitus, *Annals* iii. 43. Cf. J. J. Hatt, *Histoire de la Gaule romaine* (Paris, 1959), p. 124.

7 Tacitus, *Annals*, ii. 32.

exasperated by the suppression of the druids,[1] but almost certainly encouraged by them. We have already seen (p. 70 above) with what vehemence, almost venom, Pliny upholds the policy of the Romans in their suppression of the druids, acclaiming it as a benefit to humanity. His attitude in this matter is the more remarkable as he defines the druids as *genus vatum medicorumque*, and one would certainly have expected their medical practices at least to have commended them to Pliny. In the passage in question he tells us that the Emperor Tiberius, by a decree of the senate, put an end to the druids and that class of seers and doctors (*namque Tiberii Caesaris principatus sustulit druidas eorum et hoc genus vatum medicorumque*);[2] yet according to Pomponius Mela they continued to teach in caves (*in specu*) and hidden glades (*in abditis saltibus*).[3]

Finally, Claudius in A.D. 54 is stated by Suetonius (writing in the following century) to have 'completely abolished the barbarous and inhuman religion (*religio*) of the druids in Gaul, which under Augustus had merely been forbidden to "Roman citizens"'.[4] It is probable that the action of Claudius against druidism was inspired by the conviction that it was a subversive political element.

Pliny tells[5] us that in the reign of Claudius a Gaulish chief (a Vocontian), who had obtained Roman 'knighthood', was put to death because, while attending a lawsuit in Rome, he was found to be keeping on his person the talisman claimed

[1] Cf. M. P. Charlesworth, *Cambridge Ancient History*, x. 644; J. J. Hatt, *Histoire de la Gaule* (Paris, 1959), p. 123.

[2] *Nat. Hist.* xxx. 4 f. See however n. 4 below.

[3] *De Chorographia*, iii. 2 (ed. cit.); cf. Lucan, i. 453 ff.

[4] Druidarum religionem apud Gallos dirae immanitatis et tantum civibus sub Augusto interdictam Claudius penitus abolevit (Suetonius, *Claudius*, cap. 25). Aurelius Victor also attributes the suppression of the druids to Claudius (*De Caesaribus*, iv). Haarhoff suggests (*Schools of Gaul*, Oxford, 1920, p. 15) that in attributing the suppression of the druids to Tiberius, Pliny is guilty of a confusion: Claudius' first name being Tiberius. See further A. Momigliano, *Claudius the Emperor and his Achievement*; transl. by W. D. Hogarth (Oxford, 1934), pp. 28, 92.

[5] *Nat. Hist.* xxix. 12 *E Vocontiis*; but the reading is uncertain. For text and variants see Zwicker, op. cit. i, p. 57; cf. also Pliny, *Nat. Hist.*, ad loc. note *b* and references.

by the druids as the giver of victory in the law-courts, and known as the 'serpent's egg'. As Momigliano points out, even if the incident is fictitious, the anecdote is important as showing that this would have been a time when it would have been a punishable offence for anyone, above all a 'Roman', to support superstitions even remotely connected with druidism.[1] Even towards the close of the century, after the death of Vitellius in A.D. 69, we still hear of the druids inciting the Gauls (*Druidae canebant*) to a great national rising, seeking to persuade them by their declamations 'of vain superstition' (*superstitione vana*), in which they made reference to past history, that the nations 'on their side of the Alps' were 'destined to become masters of the world'[2] (cf. p. 46 above). This reference to the druids by Tacitus is of great importance, for it suggests that their prestige and their influence were still strong, and that imperial efforts to suppress them had not been wholly successful. After this we hear no more of the druids as an organized body, but it is unlikely that they would completely disappear quickly. It is probably about this time that they habitually carried on their functions, and especially their teaching, in sequestered places and so became invested in an atmosphere of mystery and magic. This question of policy by Rome had been a matter of lively debate ever since the foreign campaigns of Alexander, and would naturally continue among the Romans, especially after the conquests of Caesar in Gaul and the West generally.

It is interesting to note the impassioned comments against the druids with which our authorities refer to their suppression. As we have seen, Suetonius, in reference to the measures under Augustus and Claudius, calls the *religio druidarum* a *religio dirae immanitatis*. For Tacitus it is *saeva* (cf. p. 70 above); for Pliny its abolition was a benefit to humanity. Whatever the truth of these strictures all these writers express themselves with something like a heat or emotion unusual in recording contemporary legal measures, as if they felt

[1] Op. cit., p. 92.

[2] Tacitus, *Histories*, iv. 54.

themselves impelled to defend a point of view possibly controversial. May we suspect a contemporary controversy in Rome in regard to the foreign policy towards the treatment of subject peoples?

Viewed in the context of the politics of the Empire at this time, with Gaul recently conquered, the proscription of their most intellectual subversive class seems natural enough; but in 1938 N. J. de Witt published a study[1] in which he adduced some cogent arguments tending to show that the druids were never at any point during Caesar's campaigns a formidable force in Gaulish politics. He points out that in the narrative part of Caesar's warfare in Gaul, where Caesar is writing simply as a campaigner, the druids are never mentioned; the reason being, so de Witt argues, that they were no longer a force in Gaul. It is only later, in Book vi, when Caesar embarks on an excursus on the Teutons and the Gauls, that he includes a general account of the druids. His material here may be—as indeed we are already agreed—largely borrowed from an older source, probably Posidonius. Tierney also stresses (p. 214) the fact that despite the astounding powers which Caesar here ascribes to the druids he never mentions them again.

De Witt claims, no doubt rightly, that the true floruit of the druids as a powerful organized force in Gaul was long past in Caesar's day, and that it belonged to a time when Gaul was more or less unified, before 121 B.C. when the pan-Gallic league, led by the Arverni, was destroyed by Rome, and before the Barbarian invasions. In Caesar's time Gaul was split into warring factions, and the picture of 'idealized druidism' belongs rather to the period when the relative peace and unity of Gaul made a pan-Gaulish organization possible, and de Witt points out that the druids were known to the Greek world more than a century before Caesar's time. While readily allowing the historical soundness of these views

[1] 'The Druids and Romanization', *Transactions and Proceedings of the American Philological Association*, lxix (1938), pp. 319 ff.

we cannot doubt that, like the Gaulish anti-Roman Aeduan king Dumnorix, the druids had ample scope in Gaul for underground political activities in the interests of militant conservative Gaulish nationalism, and that they continued to exert their influence on the Gaulish youths sent to them for their education. As time went on the scope of the druids would inevitably weaken, especially with the development of the romanizing educational policy of Augustodunum and other Roman schools in Gaul, and the more direct proscription of druidism which we can trace briefly from Augustus to Claudius.

J. Vendryes puts the position of the subversive activities of the druids very succinctly. 'Dès la conquête terminée, le druidisme devait porter ombrage aux vainqueurs, parce qu'il représentait une force d'opposition. C'est en lui que s'incarnaient les traditions nationales. Il fallait le supprimer pour romaniser le pays.'[1]

And he points out[2] that whenever the Roman power was threatened in Gaul the druids raised their heads. This may well have been what provoked the measure of Tiberius against the druids after the revolt of Sacrovir in 21.[3] And it was certainly the case in 71, when, as a result of the revolt of Civilis, the druids preached resistance, prophesying the imminent end of the Roman Empire.[4]

Modern scholars have concerned themselves much with what is commonly referred to as 'the suppression of the druids', and have speculated widely and differed considerably as to the cause, as we have seen. It may perhaps be suggested that both these matters have come to achieve a spurious importance. What, after all, does our evidence for the actual 'suppression' amount to? Very little indeed! We have no texts or records of the promulgation of the Roman senatus in this matter, and no references in contemporary or later Roman statesmen of the first rank. Our only direct

[1] J. Vendryes, *La Religion des Celtes*, p. 294. [2] Loc. cit.
[3] Tacitus, *Annals*, iii. 40. [4] Id., *Histories*, iv. 54.

information comes from three references, two by the historian Suetonius, and one by Pliny, the value of which is, as we have remarked (p. 73, n. 4 above) uncertain. All these references are couched in terms which make us hesitate to interpret them with complete confidence, though we need not doubt that they are based on some form of Roman legislation in the first century A.D. which reacted unfavourably on the druids.

Whether suppression of the druids was the specific object of the later legal measures attributed by Suetonius and Pliny to Tiberius and Claudius respectively we do not know, in the absence of direct information of the text of the measures themselves. Clearly it was the intention of Suetonius to assure us that this was so, and the same may probably be inferred from Pliny also in so far as we can trust his statement. We have seen, however, that no direct 'proscriptive' measure against the druids is imputed to Augustus, and in the absence of a relevant document, and in view of the violent animus against the druids expressed by both Suetonius and Pliny, we must withhold judgement as to how far active persecution of the druids actually took place by Roman legislation. On the whole it must be confessed that our authorities tell us very little about both the proscriptive legislation against the druids and its actual implementation.

It is to be suspected that modern scholarship has tended to exaggerate the official suppression of the druids. The druids were doomed in the natural course of things to lose their prestige, and even their identity, with the spread of Roman culture and Roman institutions in Gaul, following on the Roman conquest. The traditional functions of the druids and their superficial philosophy, their oral poetry and teaching, their whole archaic and peripheral culture were bound to give way before the new education on Roman models, the increase in the use of writing and all the entrée to the wider world which education brought to Gaul. The young Gaulish nobility now had a life open to them in the enlightened and powerful sphere of the Roman Empire. Naturally and inevitably the druids gradually withdrew to carry on their provincial intellectual life and teaching in the secret recesses of woods and caves, no longer in Bibracte and Toulouse.

We would gladly know to what extent druidism survived after the first century A.D. It is to be suspected that its influence on the Gaul of the following centuries was still active; but in our attempt to estimate it we are once more faced with the difficulty of distinguishing between what was specifically characteristic of the druids, and what was inherently characteristic of Gaulish culture as a whole. Perhaps the distinction is here more apparent than real, if we accept the statements of the ancients that the druids were the repositories of the ancient traditions and the educators of the young. We recall their proficiency in eloquence, and the pre-eminence of the Gauls in rhetoric and poetry in the Roman world of the first century B.C., and the following centuries.[1] Again we note that the earliest schools of learning established by the Romans on Gaulish soil were in the neighbourhood of ancient Gaulish sanctuaries such as *Tolosa* (Toulouse), and later *Burdigalia* (Bordeaux), or in regions where the druids had been especially strong, e.g. Bibracte, refounded under the Romans as *Augustodunum* (Autun), while the ancient sanctuary of the god Lug, known as *Lugudunum* (Lyons), became celebrated for its rhetorical contests.

We hear nothing of druidesses in our early authorities. We may here refer to British women of the Island of *Mona* (Anglesey) described by Tacitus in his account of the attack

[1] On this subject see Sir Samuel Dill, *Roman Society in the Last Century of the Western Empire* (London, 1933), *passim*. It has already been pointed out that the groves 'devoted to cruel superstitions demolished by the conqueror' (cf. p. 30 above) are not necessarily directly associated with the druids. We have seen that sacred groves are a common feature of heathen Gaul, and that it was reported to be a common Gaulish custom to sacrifice their enemies, taken in war, for purposes of divination. Is Tacitus here using such literary sources?

by Suetonius Paulinus.[1] Tacitus refers to them here as running about among the soldiery, dressed in funeral garments like Furies, with hair streaming, carrying torches, while hard by (*circum*) druids poured forth maledictions with hands raised to Heaven. These women are not said to be druidesses, however, and nothing in the passage suggests that their behaviour differed from that of Gaulish women who are stated elsewhere[2] to have commonly taken part in battle. The comparison with Furies[3] is a natural enough literary simile for the unwonted spectacle, as reconstructed for us by the Roman Tacitus.

In an interesting passage by Pomponius Mela mention is made[4] of nine virgin priestesses on the island of Sena off the coast of Armorica (later known as Brittany) opposite the shores of the Osismii, who know the future and give oracles to sailors who come to consult them.[5] There is, however, no suggestion that these women were druidesses. Among the Teutonic tribe of the Bructeri we hear of a prophetess in the time of Vespasian (A.D. 69–79) called Veleda, which is a Celtic word connected with the root **gwel*, 'to see' (cf. Irish *fili*, 'poet'), and *Veleda* seems to be a common noun meaning 'seeress', treated as a proper name, and to have been a kind of oracle. Tacitus describes her as *virgo*, 'a maiden', and as ruling over wide territory, and as being venerated as an oracle throughout Germany. Like the druids, she was a force in politics, and her name rose to the highest pitch in

[1] Stabat pro litore diversa acies, densa armis virisque, intercursantibus feminis, quae in modum Furiarum veste ferali, crinibus deiectis faces praeferebant; Druidaeque circum, preces diras sublatis ad coelum manibus fundentes, novitate adspectus perculere militem (Tacitus, *Annals*, xiv. 30).

[2] See, e.g., Ammianus Marcellinus, v. 1. 12.

[3] The expression *in modum Furiarum veste ferali* signifies their black garments, though Tacitus may not be averse to heightening his picture with overtones by referring to the Furies. For the variant manuscript readings of the passage *deiectis faces . . . circum*, see the text edited by E. Koestermann (Leipzig, 1960), p. 312, notes 8, 9.

[4] *De Chorographia*, iii. 6.

[5] In the manuscripts they are called *Gallizenas*, *Gallicenas*, *Galligenas*. Sir John Rhŷs (*Lectures on Celtic Heathendom* (London, 1898), pp. 195 f.) explains as *Galli Senas*, an explanation which Jullian (op. cit. ii. 110) is inclined to accept. Cf. the *Gallicanas dryadas* of Vopiscus, p. 81 below, and references.

consequence of her prediction of the success of her countrymen and the destruction of the Roman legions. Later, she was chosen to represent her tribe and to arbitrate with Civilis; but the ambassadors were not admitted to her presence. In order, we are told, to increase the veneration in which she was held she lived at the top of a high tower, and all access to her was denied, a near relative being chosen to convey the questions to her, and to bring back oracular responses, 'like a messenger to a god'.[1] Tacitus speaks[2] also of other prophetic women who had preceded Veleda, and who were hardly less highly venerated, among them a certain Aurinia or Albrinia.[3] Again, Dio Cassius refers[4] to a certain inspired virgin called Ganna, among the Celts, who had succeeded Veleda (*παρθένος ἦν μετὰ τὴν Οὐελήδαν ἐν τῇ Κελτικῇ θειάζουσα*), and who is said to have accompanied Masyos, king of the Semnones, on a mission to the Emperor Domitian, and after an honourable reception by him, to have returned home.

We have, however, some slight evidence for a class of woman referred to as *dryades* (sing. *dryas*) as late as the third century A.D., and the name is probably connected with a graphic form of the word *druid*. One of these women, described as a *mulier dryas*, is stated by Lampridius[5] to have foretold defeat to Alexander Severus, prophesying in the Gaulish language, as he was setting out on a military expedition. According to Vopiscus, the Emperor Aurelianus

[1] Tacitus, *Histories*, iv. 61, 65; v. 22, 24. Cf. *Germania*, cap. 8.

[2] *Germania*, cap. 8.

[3] For the form of the name, see Pauly–Wissowa, *R.-E.*, vol. i, s.v. *Albruna*.

[4] lxvii. 12. 5 (3). The name *Ganna* is unknown elsewhere, but the form seems to be Teutonic, possibly a diminutive derived from a compound with *gand*—which in Early Norse is not rare, and is used to indicate some kind of supernatural practice, though the meaning is very obscure. Förstemann compares the place-name *Kananbrug*. For a discussion of Ganna and its affinities, see E. Förstemann, *Altdeutsches Namenbuch*, Bd. I (Bonn, 1900), cols. 593 f., s.v. *gan*; and cf. M. Schönfeld, *Wörterbuch der altgermanischen Personen- und Völkernamen* (Heidelberg, 1911), s.v.

[5] Aelius Lampridius, *Severus Alexander*, lx. See extracts from the *Scriptores Historiae Augustae*, in J. Zwicker, *Fontes Historiae Religionis Celticae*, i (Berlin, 1934), p. 97.

consulted 'Gaulish druidesses' (*Gallicanas dryadas*) on the future of his posterity.[1] According to the same writer, another woman of the Tungri (cf. modern Tongres, near Liège in Belgium), who is referred to as a druidess (*dryadas*), is said to have promised the Empire to Diocletian.[2] The last incident is particularly interesting since Tongres lies in an area for which we have no other information of this kind. These references are also interesting as suggesting that the word and the conception persisted—at least in tradition—as late as the third century, despite the interdictions referred to above. The word *dryas* appears to have survived in a slightly modified form in the proper name, *Dryadia*, the maternal aunt of Ausonius, a century later.[3] Finally it is interesting to note the traditional association of these Gaulish prophetic women with political matters. On the other hand their connexion with the druids and their *disciplina* is at most very tenuous, and Kendrick[4] is probably right in his conjecture that the name has lost is original significance.

Unfortunately our sources in regard to these 'druidesses' are far from satisfactory. All those with a national interest occur in the much-questioned document known as the *Historia Augusta*, which has been described as 'generally damned and generally used',[5] and which purports to be a collection of *Lives* of the Roman Emperors[6] written by six authors, two of whom are here referred to as Lampridius and Vopiscus.[7] The *Lives* are certainly not all of one period or by

[1] Vopiscus, *Aurelianus*, xliv; for the text see Zwicker, op. cit., p. 98, and for the alternative *Gallizenas* and for *Gallicanas*, loc. cit., n. 9; cf. also p. 79, n. 5 above.

[2] Vopiscus, *Numerianus*, xiv; for the text see Zwicker, op. cit., vol. i, p. 98.

[3] Ausonius, *Parentalia*, no. xxv.

[4] Op. cit., pp. 95 f.

[5] See E. K. Rand, *The Cambridge Ancient History*, vol. xii (Cambridge, 1939), pp. 598, 783.

[6] A recent edition with English translation is that of D. Magie, *Scriptores Historiae Augustae* in three volumes (London and New York, 1922–32). The Introduction to vol. ii contains a valuable discussion of the authorship and date.

[7] Seeck regarded *Vopiscus* as a fictitious name applied by 'the forger'—as he believed—'of the *Historia Augusta*', Pauly–Wissowa, *R.-E.*, s.v., vol. xii. 1, col. 586. See, however, Magie, op. cit. i, p. xiv. It may be added that the theory of basic forgery is now generally discredited.

one author. Probably the nucleus was made in the time of Diocletian, incorporating older material, and was completed in the fourth century.

From Ausonius we gather that even in the fourth century the druids were still a living tradition, and the Greek origin of their culture, which is vouched for by their use of the Greek alphabet—if Caesar's testimony is reliable in this respect[1]—is stressed in their proper names. Ausonius tells us[2] that Phoebicius, *aedituus* or 'temple priest' of the great Gaulish god Belenus[3] at Bordeaux, and the grandfather of Ausonius' own contemporary, Delphidius, was descended from a famous druid stock of Bayeux in Armorica (Brittany). Phoebicius, finding that he got no profit from his calling, became a teacher in the university of Bordeaux by the influence of his son, Attius Patera, himself a famous rhetorician with a great gift of eloquence. Delphidius, the son of this same Patera, was even more famous for his eloquence, and had probably been a teacher of Ausonius himself. The Delphic tradition perhaps survived in Belenus, who is traditionally equated with Apollo, and this tradition continued also in the name of Phoebicius, and in those of his son and grandson, Delphidius and Patera. We note how the tradition of poetry and eloquence is transmitted from generation to generation in this druidical family.[4] Greek names occur also in the family of Ausonius himself (cf. p. 102 below); and even the maternal grandfather of Ausonius, banished under Victricius and the two Tetrici to Tabellae (the modern Dax) on the Adour for his part in the rising of the Aedui, practised astrology in secret,[5]

[1] It is relevant to refer here to the evidence for the knowledge and use of Greek among a certain class of the Gaulish nobility cited by Jan Filip, *Celtic Civilization and its Heritage* (English translation, p. 82).

[2] In his poem commemorating the Professors of Bordeaux, *Commemoratio Professorum Burdigalensium.*

[3] For Belenus see the brief study by J. Gourvest, *Ogam*, vi (1954), pp. 257 ff.; J. de Vries, *Keltische Religion* (Stuttgart, 1961), p. 72 and *passim.*

[4] For further details of this family who claimed descent from the druids of Bayeux, see Nora K. Chadwick, *Poetry and Letters in Early Christian Gaul* (London, 1955), pp. 30 ff.

[5] See the poem of Ausonius, *Parentalia, passim.*

and may have been a descendant of druid stock.[1] The druids, as we have seen, were particularly strong in the country of the Aedui.

In Ireland we hear of druidesses (*bandruaid*), and more frequently of *banfháith*, 'seeresses', 'prophetesses', and *banfhilid*, 'poetesses'; but there seems to be no clear distinction between the use of the two latter terms. The *fili*, whose name is derived from a root **gwel*, 'to see', is represented in Irish literature as capable of attaining supernatural vision. The word *fáith*, 'prophet', 'seer' is etymologically related to Latin *vates*.[2] But these technical terms appear to be restricted to early literary usage in Ireland and we hear of no corresponding classes in Gaul.[3]

[1] For a fuller treatment of this interesting fourth-century echo of the druids reference may again be made to E. Bachelier, 'Les Druides en Gaule romaine', III 'Le Druidisme au IVe siècle', *Ogam*, xii (1960), pp. 91 ff. Bachelier calls attention to the medical tradition in the family of Ausonius.

[2] Cf. pp. 15, n. 1; 18, n. 6 above.

[3] For a brief study of the Irish *filid*, see G. Murphy, *Éigse*, ii (1940), pp. 200 ff.

VI

The Nature and History of the Druids

WE must now make some attempt to summarize the evidence of our sources, to estimate their relative value, and to draw some conclusions as to the nature of the druids and their origin and history.

Our study of the relevant passages of Strabo, Diodorus, Caesar, Lucan, and Mela have led to the conviction that an early and well-established tradition of the druids has been derived from Posidonius. This is, in fact, the earliest information which can be regarded as authoritative. In origin it appears to date from the early part of the first century B.C. Its prestige is high in its own right, for Posidonius is known to have visited Gaul; but we have no evidence that he had any first-hand contact with, or even direct information about, druids. In any case all our information goes to indicate that the *disciplina* of the druids was already on the decline in his day. How much earlier was the period of the highest power and prestige of the druids we do not know, but it is reasonable to surmise that it was most probably at the period of the height of the Gaulish independence. This at least is what we might deduce from the elaborate political organization with which Caesar credits them, and from the intellectual pretensions accorded to them by most of our authorities. There can be no doubt at all that this Posidonian tradition is the one which made the greatest impression on the writers of the first century B.C. It is evidently closely reproduced by Strabo and Diodorus, and has made a substantial contribution also to Caesar and Mela, apparently also to Lucan. We are especially indebted to it for the 'darker' side of the druids, notably their presence at human sacrifices, and also for the emphasis on the juridical functions of the druids, as well as for many of the features which they share with the Stoics and the Pythagoreans. Posidonius is not, however, solely responsible for the information of the writers of the first century B.C. From the silence of Strabo and Diodorus on the druidical teaching of the young, which is so elaborately related by Caesar, we may assume that Caesar obtained this information elsewhere.

Where is this most likely to be? No certainty is possible for us. It is most improbable that it is from his own first-hand knowledge. Pichon and others have suggested that he derived his knowledge of the teaching given by the druids from his friend the druid Divitiacus, supplemented by his own observation; but for reasons given elsewhere (pp. 48 above and 108 below), this explanation is unacceptable. Pichon may possibly be right in his suggestion that both Lucan and Mela derived their knowledge of both the teaching and the human sacrifices from the lost books of Livy.[1] This again would seem unlikely, however, for it is unsupported by either internal or external evidence relating to Livy, and Mela's debt to Caesar or his source is verbally close.

Yet another difficult and much disputed question is how far were the heirs of Posidonian tradition directly indebted to Posidonius, how far was the debt incurred through an intermediary, perhaps Timagenes of the younger generation. Timagenes is, in fact, cited from time to time by Strabo, Diodorus, and Ammianus. We have seen that while it has been claimed that Strabo's debt to Posidonius was incurred through Timagenes, there are arguments to the contrary (cf. p. 24 above). Nevertheless it can be shown that Strabo knew and made use of Timagenes. Undoubtedly Timagenes was used as a source for the druids—apparently the chief source—and was in fact held in the highest estimation by Ammianus Marcellinus. Ammianus makes no reference to the darker side of druidism, and though his notice of the druids is relatively brief, the omission suggests that this unfavourable

[1] *Les Sources de Lucain* (Paris, 1912), pp. 33 f.

aspect was either unknown to, or at least not adopted by, Timagenes. This is, indeed, one of the strong arguments against his having been an intermediary between Posidonius and Strabo.

Incidentally it would seem probable from the rather vague and obscure wording of Ammianus that he was aware also of earlier authorities than Timagenes who had left some record of the Gauls. His words are:

> Ancient writers, making investigations into the earliest origin of the Gauls, left our knowledge of the matter very imperfect; but at a later period Timagenes, a Greek both in diligence and language, collected from various writings matters which had long been unknown, and following his reliable guidance, we, dispelling all obscurity, will now propound them plainly and intelligibly.[1]

In addition to the Posidonian tradition there is another and an earlier writer who possibly comes in for consideration. This is Timaeus. It is very difficult to gauge the part that he may have played. Certain scholars of the last generation, notably J. B. Bury,[2] attached much importance to his authority and influence on later tradition, especially through the medium of quotation in the later writings of Alexander Cornelius Polyhistor and those of other Greek scholars of Alexandria. Unquestionably Timaeus gave important information to Diodorus[3] who frequently refers to his authority. Strabo also knew his work. Is it possible that Timaeus was in some way responsible for Caesar's information on the teaching of the young Gauls by the druids? Perhaps such a suggestion is favoured by the fact that this part of Caesar's account would seem to represent the druids at the height of their prestige, and this would be consistent with the fact that Timaeus was writing during the first half of the third century B.C. On the other hand, it would be rash to press this very tenuous hypothesis. Caesar's account of the druids' education of

[1] xv. 9. 2.

[2] *The Ancient Greek Historians* (London, 1909), p. 168.

[3] *Cambridge Ancient History*, vol. vi (Cambridge, 1927). Cf. Bury, p. 108, n.

the young Gauls, for which he is our only authority, may have come from quite other sources, possibly connected with events preceding the foundation of the Roman school at Augustodunum. Moreover Diodorus never cites Timaeus when speaking of the druids, though he makes extensive use of him as his source of information on Celtic matters generally, and it would be strange that he should omit such striking information as that of the druids' educational practices referred to by Caesar, if they were known already to Timaeus.

The most important authority on Timaeus in recent years is Richard Laqueur.[1] Towards the close of his detailed study of the historical and mythological elements in the work of Timaeus he claims that the greatness of the debt of Posidonius to Timaeus is generally recognized, and that it often amounts to verbal quotation, as he has sought to demonstrate in the earlier sections of his article. Laqueur then goes on to give it as his opinion that on the other hand the influence of Timagenes on later literature has been much overrated in recent times, and that Timaeus was the chief original authority of the authors who followed, and of those who made reference to Timagenes.

In what is now the standard edition of the extant fragments of Timaeus, Felix Jacoby has made a complete corpus of the surviving fragments of his writings, and an authoritative study.[2] In addition to these known and accepted fragments, Laqueur, in his detailed study referred to above, has attempted to isolate and attribute to Timaeus on linguistic grounds and other data a large amount of additional material in the work of later authors, notably Diodorus Siculus. The result of Laqueur's scholarly and exhaustive analysis has not added certainty to all the passages which he claims to be derived from Timaeus; and despite the heavy

[1] See his learned and comprehensive article in Pauly–Wissowa, *R.-E.*, 2nd series, vol. vi. 2 (1936), cols. 1076 ff., s.v.

[2] See *F. Gr. Hist.* III B. i (Leiden, 1955), no. 566, pp. 527 ff. For the texts see especially pp. 592 ff.; III B. ii (Leiden, 1955), no. 566, pp. 311 ff.

debt which Diodorus himself acknowledges to Timaeus, there were of course other historians of Sicily prior to Timaeus, and Diodorus, a Sicilian and a historian himself, could not have been ignorant of these.[1]

The great influence of the Sicilian histories of Timaeus on later writers, and on Diodorus in particular, is never in question however. His interest in general ethnographical matters, including some of the Celtic peoples, is also recognized; but it does not appear either from the extant fragments or from any specific reference of Diodorus that Timaeus had interest in, or even knowledge of the druids. Of course our knowledge of his work is only fragmentary. He may have written on the druids and the passages may have been lost. Yet if this were so it is again surprising that no hint of this should have been given, especially by Diodorus, who writes at length and in detail on the Celts, and who made liberal use of the work of Timaeus in other respects. Druids are the kind of subject in which we might expect that Timaeus might have had some superficial interest. In fact, however, we are without evidence that he made any reference to them. The question as to the possibility of his authority for the druids behind the work of Posidonius or Timagenes must be left a matter of doubt. Pliny makes frequent reference to Timaeus, especially in connexion with geographical matters (cf. p. 33 above), but never in connexion with druids.

An insuperable difficulty confronts the student working in these earliest sources, now available to us chiefly in fragments, and in the analyses made by modern scholars tracing lost texts in writings of the successors of these early authorities no longer extant. This difficulty lies in the fact that the most reliable specialists in the field are not in agreement on the nature and extent of the contribution of the earliest authorities.

[1] Cf. T. S. Brown, *Timaeus of Tauromenium* (University of California Press, 1958). See especially pp. 21, and 117, note 5. See further F. Jacoby, *F. Gr. Hist.* III B. i, no. 566, pp. 526 ff.

As already stated above, Laqueur, whose study of Timaeus is still the most authoritative—however other scholars may differ from him in certain details of interpretation—assures us categorically in his concluding remarks that the greatness of the debt of Posidonius to Timaeus is generally recognized, and that in fact—so Laqueur claims to have demonstrated—this debt is often obviously a verbal one.

Tierney, on the other hand, in his study of Posidonius, pays hardly any attention to Timaeus. In referring (p. 192) to ethnographers who preceded Posidonius he refers to Trüdinger's analysis of the ethnographic remains of Timaeus, and of Agatharchides, in which he says Trüdinger has shown that their methods are not unlike those of Posidonius, and that, in fact, Posidonius was influenced by both. But in fact Trüdinger's discussion of the work of Timaeus in this passage[1] is very brief and general. Tierney himself mentions Timaeus once later in his thesis (p. 196), and here Timaeus is only referred to as the earliest ethnographer who accepted the geographical work of Pytheas on the North Sea and its islands. Elsewhere Tierney gives it as his opinion (p. 198) that 'There is very little ethnographic material in later writers on the Celts which does not come ultimately from Posidonius.' On the whole our evidence suggests that the scope and interests of Timaeus in relation to western Europe were primarily geographical, and lay rather outside such specialized local ethnographical developments as druidism.

It would seem that Tierney is probably right in claiming (p. 219) that the sketch of Gaulish origins and ethnography quoted from Timagenes by Ammianus, 'or at least the passage concerning the learned classes of the Gauls', was 'obviously taken by Timagenes from Posidonius'. We have seen, however (p. 24 above), that Tierney has given good reasons for his agreement with Laqueur—as against Klotz— that Timagenes has not been an intermediary between Strabo and Posidonius. On the whole the relationship of our earliest

[1] *Studien zur Geschichte der griechisch-römischen Ethnographie* (Basel, 1918), pp. 108 f.

sources on the ethnography of the Gauls must remain to some extent an open question. It would seem, however, that leaving aside the difficult question of Pliny's sources, our sources for knowledge of the druids as represented in our earliest extant authorities go back to two or at most three authors—Posidonius, Timagenes, and possibly Timaeus.

When, however, we turn to examine the traditions of the druids which have come down to us from the Alexandrian school we obtain a totally different picture from that of the authorities demonstrably indebted to Posidonius. In the Alexandrian tradition the entire emphasis is different. The juridical side is not emphasized, their association with the human sacrifices of the Gauls is never referred to. Druids are referred to with respect, the accent is not on their practices but on their beliefs and their philosophy and its relationship to the current Mediterranean beliefs of their day. The druids are assigned a dignified status among the classified philosophical schools of the great systems of the world. This exaltation is sometimes exaggerated beyond what a critical scrutiny will allow, as, for example, in passages where it is stated (cf. p. 61 above) that classical philosophy had its origin among the barbarian nations; or in the estimate of the precise relationship of the tenets of the druids to the Pythagoreans. Nevertheless, these Alexandrian traditions are in their general outline consistent and credible. The druids are represented as philosophers, and as such entitled to respect.

None of the Alexandrian traditions represent the work of eye-witnesses. They are the work of scholars who are making use of written records. They represent the research and compilations of the Alexandrian school of trained scholars, and though the method of presentation and the critical treatment of the sources leaves much to be desired according to the standards of modern scholarship, they represent the responsible standard of their time in regard to the collection and selection of facts, whatever the value of the conclusions which the compilers may draw from their facts. We may refer again to the scholarly instinct which led Diogenes Laertius to go back to the earliest available sources for the Pythagoreans, by-passing the large body of later literature which had developed on the subject in the intervening period (cf. p. 66 above).

These Alexandrian traditions of the philosophical, and more especially the Pythagorean, tenets of the druids, then, are worthy of our serious consideration as among our earlier druidical traditions. The uniform respect of their tone precludes their derivation from the Posidonian tradition, which is, indeed, out of the question on general grounds. Is it possible that Bury was right in attributing the origin of the tradition to Timaeus, transmitted through Timagenes? How, we must ask, are we to explain the wide discrepancies in the two principal streams of tradition which have come down to us about the druids, both the consistent 'dark' picture of the Posidonian tradition and the equally consistent more exalted intellectual picture presented in the Alexandrian tradition? What is the evidence for the age and authenticity of the Alexandrian tradition?

One of these traditions is traced back to Alexander Cornelius Polyhistor, a younger contemporary of Posidonius, but unlike him having, so far as is known, no previous experience as a traveller in Gaul, being on the contrary a scholar and compiler of earlier traditions from written sources. He is cited by name as an authority for the description of the druids of Gaul as philosophers by Clement of Alexandria, and by Origen—who may well be simply quoting Clement; and also much later by Cyril of Alexandria. His authority is claimed by these writers for bringing the teaching of the druids into relation with the Pythagoreans, whose notebooks, dating from the fourth century, Polyhistor claims to be citing (cf. p. 66 above). Apart from these incidental references to Polyhistor as an authority on the Pythagorean tenets of the druids, we have the important witness of Diogenes Laertius (cf. p. 64 above) who is our chief ancient authority on Polyhistor, but who cites as authorities on the druids Sotion of Alexandria of the early second century B.C. and another anonymous writer of the same century who quotes the *Magicus* of Pseudo-Aristotle. Apparently Diogenes is largely indebted to the work of Sotion for his information, though not at first hand; but how far he made direct use of the sources which he cites, how far he is using sources avowedly derived from them, is of relatively little importance for our purposes. The important fact for us is that the tradition which he is recording is in origin no later, and is, in fact, evidently earlier than that of Posidonius.

Alexander Polyhistor is then a direct source of the tradition of some at least of the Alexandrian Greeks. Of him Tierney says little, but would seem to attach no importance to him as a source, apparently identifying him with the Pythagorean tradition of which he regards Posidonius as the chief exponent, and the original source of the traditions of the druids. It would, however, be less than just to Tierney to stress his reserve on Polyhistor and the Alexandrian debt, since Tierney's main thesis is a reconstruction of the general Celtic ethnography of Posidonius himself, and he is concerned with the evidence for druids chiefly in so far as this is directly relevant to his main theme.

It would seem that both Timagenes and Polyhistor, younger contemporaries of Posidonius, and in addition to them the still earlier Sotion, must have given a different picture of the druids from that of Posidonius. This earlier tradition was responsible for the conception of the druids as philosophers who shared the views of the Pythagoreans. Polyhistor held them in veneration for their lofty intellectual views, which Caesar, Ammianus, and Lucan also reported, though with less emphasis. Perhaps both Caesar and Timagenes also owed their information on the national philosophy of the druidical teaching to this tradition. It is a striking fact that Polyhistor's teaching on the druids appears to have been actually at variance with that of his older contemporary Posidonius—even contrary to it. Have we unwittingly stumbled on a forgotten controversy? Did Caesar and Ammianus, and possibly Lucan, know of the work of Polyhistor, perhaps through the intermediary Timagenes?

Be this as it may, we have now found the Alexandrian tradition as well attested as the Posidonian. In view of this ancient and well attested tradition it would be unscientific to dismiss this Alexandrian view as wholly due to the love of the Alexandrians for the strange and exotic wisdom of barbarian peoples. Bias there may well be, in both the Posidonian and the Alexandrian traditions. Unfortunately the immediate sources are lost, but the later Alexandrian writers were Christians, and are not likely to have seriously falsified the tradition of the heathen druids to their advantage. Indeed the Alexandrian Christians welcomed the idea that Greek philosophy was nothing but the 'wisdom' of the barbarians. More probably the bias here, as in the Posidonian tradition, is one of emphasis and selection. Questions of debate, following on the new knowledge of barbaric peoples acquired, first after Alexander's conquests in the East, and later after Caesar's conquest of Gaul, would inevitably relate to the proper treatment of subject populations as a result of the expansion of the Roman empire. What value was to be attached to the spiritual ideas and institutions of the peoples beyond the old frontiers of the Greco-Roman world, and what was the proper attitude to, and treatment suitable for them? Sources of exact information were few, and from these selection would naturally be made according to the political bias of the author making the extract.

Now Ammianus emphasizes the exalted philosophy of the druids and their Pythagorean tenets no less than the Alexandrians, referring to the druids as the chief civilizing influence of the Gauls (xv. 9. 8), and citing Timagenes as his authority for the statement. Timagenes was evidently Ammianus' chief source of information on the druids. We have no reason to suppose that he was an observer at first hand, and indeed as we have seen (p. 55 above) Ammianus tells us specifically that he was a scholar researching in written authorities.

From this it is abundantly clear that Ammianus claimed no first-hand contact with the druids either on his own behalf, or on behalf of Timagenes. Timagenes is himself evidently drawing on other writers—probably on Posidonius for the threefold division of the intellectual classes of Gaul, probably on Polyhistor or one of his sources for the exalted conception of the druids; possibly even on an earlier authority such as Timaeus, though as already stated, we are without any indication that Timaeus has left any direct evidence on the druids.

In seeking to estimate the truth about the druids from our multitude of varied sources and their interdependence it is of the first importance to watch the bias, or the climate in which the facts have been recorded. We have every reason to believe that Posidonius was directly responsible for the forbidding aspect of druidism which in some measure connected it with the widespread human sacrifices of the Gauls as recorded by our earliest extant authorities and recently emphasized by Professor Last. It is, as we have already remarked, significant that neither Strabo nor Diodorus mentions the teaching of the Gaulish youths as a function of the druids. It is clear that Posidonius is writing consistently with a general attitude in support of Roman imperialism and the Roman Empire, 'embracing', it was claimed, 'all the peoples of the known world in the commonwealth of God'.[1]

Now we know that Timagenes was a contemporary of Augustus at whose request he probably wrote his Histories. We are told also (cf. p. 71 above) that Augustus issued an edict which reflected unfavourably on the druids. A quarrel is known to have arisen between Augustus and Timagenes,

[1] Piero Treves, in the *Oxford Classical Dictionary* (1950), s.v. *Posidonius*.

as a result of which Timagenes burnt his Histories. Have we again stumbled on a later phase of the same controversy, which might explain why Timagenes, perhaps on the authority of Polyhistor or his source, gives a favourable picture of the druids whom Augustus viewed with disfavour? Is it possible that the two opposing streams of tradition relating to the druids, the darker one Posidonian, the lighter one Alexandrian, represent opposing political attitudes in regard to the foreign policy of the Romans to subject peoples? Has political controversy conditioned the bias and governed the selection of our reports on the druids from an earlier source or sources?

We have seen that the two strains of tradition of the druids—the darker side associating them with the 'cruel practices', and the fairer or intellectual side—meet in the accounts of Caesar, and after him Lucan and Mela, who stress the immortality of the soul. Though the passage in Caesar is obscure, it seems to imply that the soul passed into another state; and though this does not necessarily imply Pythagoreanism, we have seen that Caesar's contemporary Polyhistor is held by some later writers to be responsible for attributing Pythagorean doctrines to the druids. It is difficult to avoid the conclusion that we are dealing here with a common source used by Caesar and Polyhistor. The frequent mention of Timaeus as an authority in the work of Diodorus and his known interest in Celtic matters, together with his high prestige among Alexandrian writers, has suggested to some scholars (see pp. 86 f. above) that he may have been the chief ultimate source of our information on the teaching, and possibly even on the practices, of the druids. If we endorse this view we should have to suppose that later writers, through various intermediaries, have stressed such aspects of his account as accorded with their political bias, especially in regard to the foreign policy of Rome towards the conquered barbarian peoples. Whatever view we take as to Caesar's source for the teaching and philosophy of the druids, it is to be suspected that the political views of our authorities—the individual bias, prejudice, and policy—have dictated the selection of the facts which our extant writers have chosen to put before us from the mass of their earliest inherited information. Those who favoured the imperial policy of the repression of the druids—if, in fact, this is not to overstate the case—have emphasized the elements in druidical practices which could be used as propaganda to excuse the policy of suppression. The picture would seem to have been perhaps distorted by those favouring the imperial foreign policy towards subject peoples, and these writers have concentrated on the barbaric practices of the druids to the exclusion, or at least the prejudice of, their more important intellectual aspect.

It is clear that none of our informants had an extensive acquaintance with druidism at first hand, though Caesar and Cicero knew at least one druid in person, and Pliny may possibly have had some direct information. None of the information of the Alexandrians has independent value, and our information about the druids before their decline appears to be derived, with the possible exception of Pliny, from two or three lost sources—Posidonius, Timagenes, just possibly both originally indebted in whole or in part to Timaeus. But in fact we have no certain knowledge that even these lost sources had themselves first-hand information about the druids, even when they knew something at first hand about the Gauls.

It remains to inquire what positive information we can claim to have obtained about the druids by unpicking our sources at some length. Professor Tierney, the most recent investigator, concludes that the spiritual teaching of the druids is simply a superstructure of Stoic philosophy imposed on them by Posidonius himself, who claimed it as an historical picture of the druids. Posidonius, in Tierney's view, seems to have regarded the druids as comparable with other great men of the past who were theologians and lawgivers, such as Moses, and Tierney further claims that Posidonius represents them as priests, philosophers, and theologians, possessed of the highest political authority, and in charge of divination and sacrifice. Posidonius pictures them as expounding to upper-class Gauls the study of theology, ethics, and natural science, including the physics of the earth and the stars, and as holding among their main tenets that the soul of man is immortal. This, says Tierney, is not an historical picture, but rather a rhetorical one, simply a reproduction of the programme of Stoic philosophy. It is, he claims, incompatible with our information of the Gauls as head-hunters, practising divination by human sacrifice, and with our picture of Gaulish religion as represented by recent writers such as Vendryes.[1] Finally, Tierney claims that 'this priesthood was not in any way a distinguished exception among the priesthoods of the contemporary barbarian nations'.

Against this I would urge that the druids are nowhere—save perhaps in Pliny's bizarre account—represented as priests,[2] or as directly occupied with religion, and thus the characteristic features of Gaulish religion as defined by Vendryes,[3] and stressed by Tierney (p. 223), have no bearing on the philosophical or scientific pretensions of the druids. The political functions ascribed to them and their lofty intellectual teaching are quite other than the routine of religious officials or functionaries localized in relation to specific sanctuaries. Again it may be urged that the cruelties and barbaric practices of the Roman arena show that such practices are not necessarily incompatible with a high civilization. As Tierney himself allows, Posidonius was a careful observer. In his account of the teaching of the druids

[1] See J. Vendryes, *La Religion des Celtes* (Paris, 1948), pp. 239 ff.

[2] The definition of druids as priests is a common assumption by modern scholars, e.g. W. E. Heitland, *The Roman Republic* (Cambridge, 1909), iii. 158. De Vries assumes at the outset, and throughout his article ('Die Druiden', *Kairos*, ii. 67 ff.) that the druids are a priesthood. Cf., however, pp. 2, 5 ff. above.

[3] J. Vendryes, loc. cit.

he may exaggerate and even distort its tenor in accordance with his special interest in Stoicism; but he is unlikely to have given a fundamentally false presentation. Similarly Caesar may, and almost certainly does, colour his narrative for his political purpose; but he has much to tell us of interest which lies outside special pleading, whether by Caesar himself or by his source. The position of the druids may have been magnified in his accounts, as Tierney believes; but their philosophy is consistent with what we know of the so-called Pythagoreans of the Mediterranean countries of this time, and the political influence of the druids is vouched for by their later history.

It may even be conceded that not only are we practically without any first-hand information about the druids, but that all our traditional information has come to us through sources tinged with political bias. What we have been accustomed to dignify as a reliable account of the druids is a collection of facts selected according to the political views, or at best the limited outlook, environment, and opportunities of the narrator at a given time and place. Nevertheless a survey of the sum of information which has come to us, and an attempt at a critical analysis of the sources, have given us data for a tentative conclusion of some historical validity.

Our first conclusion is that in following the chronological order of our sources we are studying the druids during the period of their decline. The prestige and organization attributed to them by the earliest writers must have been built up in the period when the Gauls were a united people and before the Barbarian invasions or the Roman conquest. The military decline of the Gaulish nation, and the Roman influence on cultural matters must have inevitably and radically changed the picture. The Roman imperial edicts prejudicial to the druids as enacted by Augustus and his successors, following on the introduction of the Roman system of education among the young Gaulish nobility, could not fail to bring about a final disintegration of the whole system and *disciplina* of the druids. Intellectual disintegration must inevitably have set in. Once the central organization had been dismembered and its educational system superseded the druids would lose the dignity of the earlier large assemblies and the coherence, together with the power, of a centrally organized body, while the earlier speculative philosophy would naturally degenerate, possibly into magical practices. Driven as fugitives to woodlands and caves, the druids could now only carry on their ancient calling enshrouded in increasing mystery in the eyes of their Roman conquerors on whom we are dependent for our information. The last we hear of so-called 'druidesses'—for what the information is worth (cf. p. 81 above)—resembles the modern gypsy fortune-teller, while the last of the druids of Brittany are drafted into the romanized university of Bordeaux.

That the druids were a subversive element in the Empire is certain.[1] Their strong conservatism, their devotion to the ancient Gaulish ways of thought, can be seen in the fanatical tenacity with which they devoted themselves and their pupils to oral learning, even while making use of Greek letters in almost all other matters. Their strong nationalism is emphasized by Tacitus, and was still a serious source of trouble to the Romans as late as A.D. 71. It is perhaps no accident that *Armorica*, which retained strong traditions of druidical families within the memory of Ausonius, was the most persistently rebellious of all the western provinces, and the stronghold of the mysterious and disaffected *Bagaudae*, throughout the greater part of the fifth century.

The Romans have found themselves obliged to take active measures for the suppression of the instigators of these nationalistic and separatist movements. Yet they must have been aware that to do so was to strike at the very heart of the Gaulish people whom they were most anxious to conciliate. Active propaganda was essential to justify the Romans to

[1] Cf., e.g., C. Jullian, *La Gaule*, iii. 373 ff. and the references there cited.

themselves and to their Gaulish subjects, and to this end, from the first century B.C. onwards, they have been concerned to seek justification for repressive treatment of a proud and independent people whom they were seeking to overpower. From the time of Augustus it was realized that the education of the young Gaulish nobility must be transferred from the teaching of the druids to that of the Roman schools. Augustus accordingly very naturally forbade those who were reckoned as 'Roman citizens'—i.e. those who had acquired the status of citizenship in the Empire—to practise druidism. Very naturally also those who, like Suetonius, were concerned to uphold the policy of the emperors sought to uphold it by selecting and emphasizing the traditions of the unfavourable aspects of druidism. Accordingly Suetonius assigns the highest motives of humanity to Augustus and Claudius in their measures unfavourable to druidism. He would hardly be in a position to contradict an imperial propaganda campaign, and writing with a *parti pris* he naturally, in his brief references to the legislative measures against the druids, assigns the Gaulish religion as the imperial justification for their suppression.

Yet it is certain that it is the intellectual side of druidism which made the deepest and most lasting impression on the ancients, and which is in fact its most interesting feature. And here again we must stress the fact that it is this tradition of an intellectual class which has survived, while there is almost no evidence for ethical or moral teaching, and no hint of a system of punishments in a life after death. Similarly we would again stress the absence of local druid sanctuaries, of evidence of sacerdotal ritual or liturgy, of any interest in the known divinities of ancient Gaul. This negative evidence is important. It is the obverse of that druidical spiritual and intellectual teaching which is claimed to have had as its chief concern the nature of the physical universe (the *natura rerum*) and the nature and destiny of the human soul. These are not the characteristics of priests but of philosophers—and especially, I would add, of Greek philosophers.

The *outstanding* features of the druidical teaching may be summed up as natural philosophy and natural science—the nature of the physical universe and its relationship to mankind. This branch of human knowledge was characteristic of the early Greek philosophers of Ionia,[1] and it is probable that the druids and the seers of Gaul, representing the backward but not wholly uncultured peoples on the periphery of Greek civilization, have preserved and transmitted late echoes of early philosophy and knowledge derived from the common property of the ancient Greek world which probably penetrated Gaul in the first place through the Greek colony of Marseilles. The form of this knowledge and this philosophy which seems to have penetrated Gaul and inspired the philosophy and the teaching of the druids, was associated by the Alexandrian Greeks in particular with 'Pythagoreanism'. It is of course inconceivable that any system of philosophy was adopted by them in a pure form or that it can be traced in the work of a single teacher. But the exact nature of the West Mediterranean form of philosophy current at the formative period of the thought and teaching of the druids must be left to specialists of Greek philosophy. They it is who hold the key.

On the whole it would seem reasonable to regard the druids as barbaric survivors of ancient Mediterranean systems of education and philosophical thought, rather than to look upon them as a priesthood which was not essentially different from that of the Germani and other barbaric peoples of ancient Europe. For the latter definition and identification I can see no valid evidence. Rather I would suggest that their 'discipline' represents a peripheral and remote survival of the brilliant speculative era which had achieved its highest expression in the great Ionian philosophers of the sixth century B.C. and which penetrated the

[1] For an interesting account of the two branches, see an article by the late Professor F. M. Cornford, 'Was Ionian Philosophy Scientific?' in the *Journal of Hellenic Studies*, lxii (1942), pp. 1 ff.

more remote countries of the West, transformed by many and varied superimpositions at a later date.

How otherwise can we account for druidism by any explanation consistent with the facts? It appears, by a consensus of the evidence, to be limited to the Celts of Gaul and, perhaps at a much later date, of Ireland. We know that all the early coins of Gaul were derived from Greek models. The art of the Iron Age, known as La Tène, in Gaul and in Ireland has been widely influenced by Greek motifs. The druids in almost all their public and private correspondence are said to make use of Greek letters (*Graecis litteris utantur*). A relationship between druidism and the Greek world such as I have suggested would be consistent with the use of the Greek alphabet by the druids to which Caesar refers, and with the Greek personal names in the family of Phoebicius of druidical ancestry, as reported by Ausonius (cf. p. 82 above). The Greek colony of Marseilles, founded from Phocaea in Asia Minor *c.* 600 B.C., cannot have been without a permanent effect on the interior of Gaul.[1] Indeed we are told by Strabo[2] that it was the chief channel by which Greek education and thought entered Gaul, and taught the Gauls within its sphere of influence to become 'Philhellenes'. I would suggest that perhaps the complex of culture which we call 'druidism' is a provincial peripheral survival of ancient Greek intellectual systems carried on more or less in isolation in Gaul, and combined with early native elements on the confines of the Ancient World. This strange and interesting development has left its traces in both Gaul and Ireland, and in Gaul was recorded in early times by one or more Greek writers from whose works later Greek and Roman writers have selected their information according to their own political theories and their own more immediate needs for political propaganda.

[1] On this subject see the linguistic evidence assembled by W. von Wartburg, 'Die griechische Kolonisation in Süd-Gallien und ihre sprachlichen Zeugen im Westromanischen', *Von Sprache und Mensch*. See also Jan Filip, *Celtic Civilization and its Heritage* (English translation), pp. 38, 51, 77, and *passim*.

[2] v. I. 15.

NOTE

Divitiacus and Dumnorix

REFERENCE has been made above to Divitiacus,[1] a most interesting figure and a friend of both Caesar and Cicero. Both refer to him, and have left us, in fact, our only contemporary portrait of a druid. He was a chief of the Aedui, the most advanced and the most romanized of the Gaulish provinces, with its capital on the Gaulish hill-fort of Bibracte, which later gave place (*c.* 12 B.C.) to Augustodunum (cf. p. 71 above). His younger brother Dumnorix seems to have been in power when Divitiacus first comes before us as a political figure. Dumnorix, however, was a steadfast nationalist, and the leader of the anti-Roman party among the Aedui, whereas Divitiacus was a loyal and devoted adherent of the Roman imperial policy.

About 71 B.C. Ariovistus, the king of the Teutonic tribe of the Suebi, invaded Gaul, induced by the Gaulish tribe of the Sequani, and defeated their rival Gaulish tribe the Aedui. The chief magistrate (*vergobret*) of the Aedui, the druid Divitiacus, went to Rome *c.* 60 B.C., and made an impassioned appeal to the senate for help for his tribe against the Teutonic invader.[2] In a Latin panegyric of uncertain authorship addressed to Constantine the Great, Divitiacus is recalled to us in retrospect, though not by name, as 'the Aeduan prince, haranguing the senate, leaning on his long shield' (*scutum*)[3]—a picturesque and characteristic Gaulish orator.

[1] A Celtic name which appears in various forms in manuscripts, and in an inscription in Lyons in the form Diviciac[us] (*Corpus Inscript. Lat.*, vol. xiii, no. 2081). I have employed the form of the name which has become familiar through long usage.

[2] Caesar, *Gallic War*, i. 31; vi. 12. The references to Caesar throughout the following pages are to the *Gallic War* unless otherwise stated.

[3] Princeps Aeduus ad senatum venit, rem docuit, cum quidem oblato

His mission was in vain, however. In 59 B.C., the year of Caesar's consulship, the senate recognized Ariovistus as 'king' and 'friend of the Roman people' (*rex atque amicus*),[1] probably at Caesar's suggestion. Caesar in fact refers to him as *rex Germanorum*.[2]

It was doubtless during this mission to Rome that Divitiacus made the acquaintance of Cicero and probably of Caesar also.[3] Cicero refers to him simply as a druid, without any mention of his political interests. His passage is as follows:

> The system (*ratio*) of divination is not even neglected among barbaric peoples, since in fact there are Druids in Gaul; I myself knew one of them, Divitiacus of the Aedui, your guest[4] and eulogist, who declared that he was acquainted with the system (*ratio*) of nature which the Greeks call natural philosophy (φυσιολογία) and he used to predict the future by both augury and inference.[5]

From now onwards our chief guide of the actual course of events in Celtic Gaul, and of the part played by Divitiacus and his brother Dumnorix, is Caesar's *Gallic War*. Dio Cassius, who covers in more general terms the course of Caesar's campaign in Gaul at this period in Books xxxviii. 3–xxxix. 5 adds little to the general picture and makes no reference to Divitiacus or Dumnorix.

From Caesar we learn that after the conquest of the Aedui, Ariovistus and the Germans continued to spread through Gaul, overcoming all resistance. In 61 B.C. a section of the nobility of the powerful Gaulish tribe of the Helvetii, under the leadership of Orgetorix, the head of the Helvetian nobles, formed a conspiracy and threatened invasion of Roman territory in the Gaulish province. Orgetorix was

concessu minus sibi vindicasset quam dabatur, scuto innixus peroravit (*Panegyrici Latini*, no. v (3), ed. Baehrens (Leipzig, 1911), p. 190; *Panégyriques latins*, text and translation by E. Galletier, ii (Paris, 1952), pp. 91 f.).

[1] Caesar, i. 35.

[2] Caesar, i. 31.

[3] Cicero, *De Divinatione*, i. 41. See W. E. Heitland, *The Roman Republic*, vol. iii (Cambridge, 1909), p. 163, footnote.

[4] The person addressed is Cicero's brother, Quintus. The *De Divinatione* is composed in the form of a dialogue between Cicero and Quintus at Cicero's country house at Tusculum.

[5] Cicero, *De Divinatione*, cap. 41.

joined by Casticus, son of the king of the Sequani, and by Dumnorix, brother of Divitiacus, and son-in-law to Orgetorix, and himself the powerful leader of the anti-Roman party among the Aedui. The Aedui counted officially among the allies of the Romans, and in fact the loyalty of Divitiacus himself to Rome never wavered.[1]

Both Orgetorix and Dumnorix hoped to make themselves independent kings, and to restore the independence of Gaul. The conspiracy failed, and the Helvetii repudiated Orgetorix, who died before they could punish him for the treason of which they accused him; but the Helvetii nevertheless made up their minds to migrate *en masse* from their mountain home in Switzerland to the richer lands of south-western Gaul.[2] With some other tribes they began to march through Gaul, overrunning the Aedui before Caesar could protect them, or meet the Helvetii in a general encounter. In fact in Caesar's progress northwards he was sorely hampered by disaffection among the Aedui themselves, which was strongly and persistently fostered by Dumnorix. He, by his wealth and munificence and skilful diplomacy with the neighbouring tribes and his strong nationalist sympathies, now possessed more power with the Aedui than the official magistrates, Divitiacus and Liscus. 'He hated Caesar and the Romans',[3] and was aiming at revolution, holding that if the Aedui could no longer possess the primacy among the Gaulish states, it would be better to be ruled by Gauls than by Romans.

In accordance with his general anti-Roman and pro-Helvetian policy, and without the consent or knowledge of his own magistrates or of Caesar, Dumnorix induced the Sequani to allow the migrating Helvetii to pass through their territory with the purpose of settling in Roman Gaul. Moreover in order to hamper Caesar's progress northwards against the Helvetii he induced the Aedui to withhold the corn

[1] Caesar, i. 3.

[2] On the implications of the conspiracy, see J. J. Hatt, *Histoire de la Gaule romaine*, 50.

[3] Caesar, i. 18.

supplies sorely needed by Caesar, and to keep the Helvetii informed of what took place in Caesar's camp. Finally, so we are informed, he caused Caesar's cavalry, of which he commanded Aeduan levies, to miscarry when sent to cut off the advance of the Helvetii. His entire anti-Roman activities and the means by which he was enabled to fulfil his aims were reported to Caesar in a private interview between the Aeduan magistrate Liscus and Caesar.[1] Dumnorix was clearly due for trial, but Caesar was in a serious difficulty owing to the undoubted loyalty of Divitiacus the brother of Dumnorix. In a speech which Caesar claims to report verbatim Divitiacus asserted that it had been by his help that his younger brother had come to power, and that in view of his own friendship with Caesar the severe punishment of Dumnorix would alienate from Divitiacus the public feeling of all Gaul. Accordingly he begged and obtained pardon for Dumnorix from Caesar.[2] In fact, the general situation as represented to us in Caesar's narrative left Caesar no choice.

Caesar states specifically that this interview between himself and Divitiacus took place through an interpreter; and indeed it is commonly stated by modern scholars that Divitiacus never acquired the use of the Latin tongue. This, however, is hardly a warrantable conclusion from a diplomatic discussion on such mighty issues. All that we can say with certainty is that the Latin of Divitiacus at this stage was at best imperfect.

Caesar tells us that although he extended pardon to Dumnorix he had him watched,[3] but from this time, so far as we can accept Caesar's account, the prestige of Divitiacus seems to have been paramount, not only among his own people, but also among the Gaulish chiefs as a whole. After Caesar's eventual defeat of the Helvetii in 58 B.C. he claims that a convention of the chiefs of nearly all of the Gaulish states besought his help against the growing power of Ariovistus and the Teutonic invaders.

[1] Caesar, i. 17, 18. [2] Ibid. i. 19, 20. [3] Ibid. i. 20.

'Divitiacus the Aeduan spoke for them', and a full account of his long oration is again reproduced by Caesar as verbatim.[1]

Later in the year Divitiacus—the one Gaul[2] in whom Caesar had complete faith—lent important help to Caesar in his march against Ariovistus and the Belgae by guiding his army through difficult terrain.[3]

In Caesar's account of the struggle against the Belgae in 57 B.C. we get a revealing glimpse of his technique in negotiating with Divitiacus, again as reported by Caesar himself: he tells us that during his campaign against Ariovistus he made a pressing appeal to Divitiacus, representing to him how great an advantage it would be for both Romans and the Aedui to keep apart the two main bodies of the enemy—the Belgae and the Bellovaci.

'This', continued Caesar, 'could be done if the Aedui led their own forces into the borders of the Bellovaci and began to lay waste their lands', and he concludes cryptically: 'With these instructions he dismissed him' (*his mandatis eum ab se dimittit*).[4]

The result is well known. The Belgae continued resistance but in vain, and on hearing of the approach of Divitiacus and the Aedui against the borders of their allies the Bellovaci, the entire resistance crumbled.[5] It may be noted that it is nowhere stated that Divitiacus himself took an active personal part in the fighting, or that Caesar asked that he should do so, though either is possible.

Finally after Caesar's defeat of the Belgae, to which Divitiacus had contributed by his prompt measures against their allies the Bellovaci, Divitiacus again made an eloquent and highly diplomatic appeal to Caesar for pardon towards the Bellovaci, near neighbours of the Aedui, to whom they were closely united by common interest against the Belgae. Again Caesar reports the speech verbatim and replied that 'For the

1. Ibid. i. 31, 32.
2. Reading *ex Gallis*; or perhaps better *ex aliis*; cf. Klotz, ed. cit. i. 41, l. 26.
3. Caesar, i. 41.
4. Ibid. ii. 5.
5. Ibid. ii. 10.

respect which he had towards Divitiacus and the Aedui he would receive them [i.e. the Belgae] into his protection.'[1]

It is evident that oratory was one of the chief accomplishments, even functions, of Divitiacus. Apart from the impressive reference by the panegyrist to his speech before the Roman senate, Caesar himself concludes his own account of each crisis in his Gaulish campaign with a verbatim report of a speech by Divitiacus, always diplomatic in content and astute in argument. It will be recalled that these speeches occur in Caesar's narrative (1) after the subversive tactics of Dumnorix with the purpose of hindering Caesar's advance against the Helvetii; (2) in the passage in which the Gaulish chiefs are represented as uniting in their appeal to Caesar through the mouth of Divitiacus for help against the advance of Ariovistus; (3) after the defeat and retreat of the Belgae and their allies, more especially the Bellovaci. We know, of course, that these speeches cannot have been reported precisely as they were delivered; but their general character, the occasions to which they are assigned, and above all the astute political insight, which not even the vehemence of the professional Gaulish rhetor disguises, justify us in believing that in these speeches Caesar has given us his own direct impression of an important function of Divitiacus in Gallo-Roman politics.

Caesar nowhere refers to Divitiacus as a druid, and various conjectures have been made to explain this. Jullian thought[2] that it was in virtue of his courage and sagacity that Caesar omits to refer to him as a druid and that the panegyrist also refers to him as *princeps*. In fact in such notices of him as we have received he makes so little use of the qualities commonly attributed to the druids that one might suspect that Caesar did not know that he was a druid. There may in fact have been other druids among the chiefs whom Caesar knew. On the other hand, we need not regard Divitiacus as a typical druid but perhaps as a product of the Roman policy of 'romanizing' the young Gaulish nobility. In all probability, however,

[1] Caesar, ii. 14, 15. [2] Op. cit. ii. 93.

in view of Cicero's statement, he may well be typical of the druids at their best and in their best period, and his influence with Caesar, and the important political help which he rendered him, almost entitles him to the description of the political power ascribed to the druids by Dio Chrysostom (cf. p. 49 above).

Cicero's testimony is categorical and based on the best of evidence—his own personal knowledge of Divitiacus, and the interest which they shared in augury. Here, however, we must be careful not to go beyond Cicero's carefully worded statement. He tells us (cf. p. 47 above) that Divitiacus 'declared that he was acquainted with *naturae rationem quam φυσιολογίαν Graeci appellant* and that he used to predict the future by augury'. Cicero is reporting what he had been told by Divitiacus, not what he had himself witnessed. Moreover, Divitiacus may quite possibly have been speaking of his earlier days, before he had come under Roman influence. A final consideration is surely not without significance. In Caesar's summary and contrast[1] of the customs of Gaul and Germania, including his brief account of the predominance of the Aedui among the Gaulish states prior to their conquest by Ariovistus, and of the mission of Divitiacus to Rome, and of the subsequent reinstatement of the Aedui by Caesar,[2] Caesar passes immediately and without further preamble to our longest and most circumstantial account of the druids.[3]

After the defeat of the Bellovaci Divitiacus disappears from the scene; but this is not the end of this interesting royal family of the Aedui. The scene shifts once more to the final act of the little drama of Dumnorix. We left him an unrepentant and staunch Gaulish nationalist, unaffected by the failure of his conspiracy with Orgetorix, and continuing to use all the resources of his accumulated wealth, popularity, and far-sighted diplomatic connexions with the anti-Roman elements among the Gaulish nobility in order to strengthen the independence of the Aedui and of Gaul. We have seen

[1] Caesar, vi. 11 f. [2] Ibid. vi. 12. [3] Ibid. vi. 13.

him secretly making use of all his resources to aid the advance of the Helvetii into Gaul and to hinder Caesar's advance against them, and we have seen that Caesar felt himself obliged to pardon him, though he had him closely watched.[1]

When in 55–54 B.C. Caesar made two expeditions into Britain he took with him on the second occasion the Gaulish chiefs whom he felt he could not safely leave behind in Gaul. Chief of these was Dumnorix whom he knew to be steadfast in his aim at revolution and the sovereignty of the Aedui, and whom he knew also to be a powerful influence among the Gauls. Caesar constantly refers to his popularity, especially among the common people,[2] and was well aware that he was already intriguing actively against him by spreading false rumours to his disadvantage.[3] Dumnorix expressed the greatest unwillingness to accompany Caesar to Britain, alleging, among other pretexts, that he was hindered by his religious responsibilities (*quod religionibus*[4] *impediri sese diceret*). This last is a very interesting hint, the first we have had that 'religious' commitments played any part in the functions of Dumnorix. Meanwhile Dumnorix continued to work upon the Gaulish chieftains, stirring them up to refuse embarkation with Caesar and urging that he and they should stand firm in executing whatever should be for the advantage of Gaul. Caesar's own account of the attitude and machinations of Dumnorix before the embarkation represents Caesar himself as in a situation calculated to cause desperate apprehension.

Finally when the moment of embarkation came Dumnorix with certain Aedui troops left the Roman camp without Caesar's knowledge and set off for home.[5] Caesar dispatched a large body of cavalry to follow him and force him to return and to put him to death if he would not submit, or resisted forcibly. Dumnorix was not the man to submit. He resisted and defended himself, calling upon the help of his followers,

[1] Caesar, i. 20. [2] Ibid. i. 3, 9, 18. [3] Ibid. v. 6.

[4] The use of the plural here is interesting. *Religio* is obviously not used here in the usual spiritual sense of 'religion'. [5] Caesar, v. 7.

and shouting repeatedly that he was a free man and of a free state. He was surrounded and slain, according to orders, and the Aedui cavalry returned to Caesar. Even seen through the hostile eyes of a Roman conqueror Dumnorix stands out as a brave and exceptionally able Gaulish chieftain, of inflexible patriotism and devotion to his native land, implacably opposed to the Roman interests in Gaul among the Aedui in particular. The contrast between the two Aeduan princes, Divitiacus and Dumnorix, could hardly be more violent. We cannot feel so certain today as we should have felt a generation ago that Divitiacus was the greater patriot.

That Divitiacus was a druid we are not left in doubt and we may accept his word that he was versed in φυσιολογία and augury, which are associated in our earliest authorities with the Gaulish druids. Whether he remained a druid after coming under Roman influence we do not know. Probably he did not. This would account for Caesar's silence on the subject, though other explanations are possible. A more difficult question arises in regard to Dumnorix. He is never stated to be a druid; but one wonders. His background is in all probability the same as his brother's. He evidently enjoyed the confidence of those Gaulish chiefs who were opposed to Caesar, and enjoyed unbounded popularity among the common people. What are the *religiones*, the 'religious responsibilities' which—so he alleged to Caesar—precluded his crossing over to Britain? His extreme conservatism and dedication to the Gaulish cause in implacable opposition to Roman influence are completely consistent with the political attitude of the druids as we gather this from later writers. In fact apart from what we learn of Divitiacus from Cicero, and surveying the evidence for druids as a whole, Dumnorix, as he comes before us in the pages of Caesar, answers more closely to our latest reports of the druids inciting the Gauls against the Roman conquerors than his elder brother.

INDEX